NAUTICAL ETIQUETTE AND CUSTOMS

Those siren songs of sea traditions,
They haven't really died.
The words perhaps have been forgotten
But the melodies abide.

They live among the memories
And lore of classic ships
As backdrop to the newer songs
Now sung from younger lips.

L.L.

NAUTICAL ETIQUETTE
AND
CUSTOMS

*

SECOND EDITION

BY LINDSAY LORD

Foreword by Waldo C. M. Johnston
With drawings by C. D. Clarke

CORNELL MARITIME PRESS
Centreville, Maryland

Library of Congress Cataloging in Publication Data

Lord, Lindsay.
        Nautical etiquette and customs.

        1. Yachts and yachting—History. 2. Etiquette.
3. Naval ceremonies, honors, and salutes—History.
I. Title.
GV826.L67   1987   395'.59   86-47716
ISBN 0-87033-356-9

Manufactured in the United States of America

First edition, 1976. Second edition, 1987

TO RUTH
my navigating officer
ashore and afloat

CONTENTS

FOREWORD

EVERY ONCE IN A WHILE a book surfaces in the maritime publishing field that commands more than casual attention. *Nautical Etiquette and Customs*, by Lindsay Lord, is such a book. It does not pretend to spellbind the reader as do *The Hunt for Red October* or *The Riddle of the Sands*; it does not induce the chills of *Heavy Weather Sailing*; it does not seek to replace Chapman as the sailor's Bible, nor does it vie with the beauty and magic of *The Sailor's World*.

Instead, Mr. Lord concentrates on a subject of concern to all experienced sailors—the knowledgeable command of a taut ship and good manners at sea. Rudeness in the drawing room may bring a reprimand or social ostracism, but poor manners at sea can result in tragedy. Today's overcrowded waterways and harbors are infested with growing numbers of clowns and macho types at the wheels of vastly overpowered motorboats they don't know how to control and at the helms of sophisticated sailboats they don't know how to maneuver. Their numbers are augmented by owners of small unseaworthy craft who overburden their boats with too many people and too much beer—and venture too far from shore with inadequate life-saving gear, without charts, without compasses, and without any concept of how dangerous and merciless the sea can suddenly and unexpectedly become.

It is these thoughts that have motivated Lindsay Lord in writing *Nautical Etiquette and Customs*. With a touch of nostalgia, a wisp of cynicism, and a lively note of humor he sketches the evolution of a strict code of ethics and conduct at sea that over the years has proven to be the best defense against disaster. He cites the rigid responsibilities of command laid on the captains of Cunard liners, which resulted in an unmatched safety record; no Cunard ship ever suffered a passenger fatality in peacetime during two centuries of transatlantic service!

Mr. Lord then traces the development of yachting manners and customs as inherited and practiced by the corinthian swells of the late 19th and early 20th centuries. Like the people and mores of the times of F. Scott Fitzgerald, many of these yachting rituals with their effusive pomp and ceremony have become archaic. These he dismisses. But the traditional elements of courtesy and prudence, and pride in the command of a well-run vessel, he retains as being as pertinent today as they have been through the centuries.

Thus *Nautical Etiquette and Customs* is a textbook of nautical courtesy—and its style of presentation makes it extremely readable. The experienced sailor will enjoy its flavor. The younger and still inexperienced sailor will find some salty advice that will improve his competence as a skipper and enhance his pride in the operation of his boat. He, and young flag officers of our yacht clubs, will gain insight in those traditions of conduct at sea and ashore that have stood the test of time and that can add much to the enjoyment and purpose of modern pleasure boating. Small though this book is, it deserves a place in the library of anyone who puts to sea.

Waldo C. M. Johnston
Director Emeritus, Mystic Seaport

PREFACE

ARLY sailors, lured by commerce, were at once fascinated and repelled by the sea and the great unknown of distant shores. They held fast to all the superstitions and customs which they hoped would somehow improve their chances of getting home alive. Then, after many centuries of explorations and experiences in the art of building ships and boats, a sporting few of the jaded aristocracy created and adopted private boating as a pleasant hobby exclusively for the upper crust. Their boats became increasingly magnificent, their showy customs followed Royal Navy protocol, and their manners emulated those of the Court—altogether an eminently satisfactory and conspicuous display of wealth and high position.

Much of this "play navy" attitude survived the social upheavals of the twentieth century's two world wars but the courtly customs have become more and more ignored and finally forgotten. The older and more influential yacht clubs continued to reprint their yearbooks with archaic bylaws still interred in the unheeded back pages, but to little effect. Instead, informality reigns. Newcomers are more relaxed, less governed by traditions. Their more casual and careless approach to all activities, the servantless society, and the use of engines in boats of every sort, finally doomed the great old customs in spite of earnest efforts by the Chapmans, the Rigges, and even the U. S. Power Squadrons, themselves an early cause of this dethroning of the past. A modern breed of skippers now ignores the old pretensions, albeit with an understandable degree of uncertainty as to what, if anything, is really correct.

Fortunately, there are indications everywhere among the more sophisticated boating people that a new code of behavior and a new pattern of amenities are appearing to fill the need. These new customs remain only to be codified and sanctioned by their general use in order that we may once again enjoy the safe and comfortable assurance of correctness; a code based on priceless background and reinforced with proven safety practices.

NAUTICAL ETIQUETTE AND CUSTOMS

CHAPTER ONE

IN THE WAKE

L ET's picture a fleet of English frigates, meeting as they often did in some outpost harbor of the colonies: majestic bulwarks of an empire encircling the world. The sun, which always shone somewhere along those wide-flung ramparts, might here be sinking to yardarm level, time for proper sociability touched with royal protocol.

A fluttering flag-hoist signal from the flagship invited senior officers throughout the fleet to come aboard and drink a "health" or two. Boats were lowered from the anchored ships and with precision strokes by white-clad sailors, the officers were wafted to the flagship. The heftier among these captains might be hoisted up in bosun chairs and piped aboard in style. That "piping" was the bosun's whistle-code instructions to the lads who hauled the falls. The highest pitch meant "haul handsomely," that is, smartly; a lower pitch was "hold"; and an artful tremolo said "slack off."

Delivered safely and assembled in the admiral's cabin, the most bemedalled seniors on the starboard side, the more junior ranks to port, they raised their glasses in a health "To the King." Thereupon a flag detail stationed at the signal halyards and a gunner's mate below reacted promptly to the raised fist of the watchman stationed at the cabin skylight. The guns roared out from all around the bay, and the echoes of this ritual rolled off among the hills.

Then came another health "To the Queen" with smoke and powder slammed across the waters and out among the farms while profound but politic opinions were being aired, each safe topic started by a senior lounging in his privileged seat to starboard, each pronouncement dutifully rephrased and even amplified by succeeding lesser ranks.

Next in sequence came a health to every lower grade of royalty, each fully cannonaded, the sweating gunners swabbing out artillery and passing ammunition. Perhaps, depending on the numbers of that royal roster or the proportionate dilution of the rum as ordered by the admiral whose private stock it was, perhaps the ranks of officers who rose to each succeeding health might be thinning out a little, but for those who stoutly carried on, there were always dukes and duchesses and earls and barons. And the cannon roared.

As Hamlet described the revelry on a similar occasion when the English ambassador received the King of Denmark on board the *Golden Lion* at Elsinor:

No jocund health that Denmark drinks today,
But the great cannon to the clouds shall tell,

This was repeated on a grand scale when the King of Denmark returned the visit. King James and his Queen were entertained on board the Danish flagship off Gravesend, and, as set forth in a history of the Court:

> At every health, there were from the ships of Denmark and the forts some three or fourscore great shot discharged, and of these thundering volleys there were between forty and fifty.

The reporter may have counted "between forty and fifty" but on the average, down through the years, it was pretty well established that very few of that tosspot gentry could struggle to their feet for even health number twenty-one. And thus it came about, fully demonstrated by great bellied gourmands, that only for the high and mighty do we now blast a twenty-one gun salutation.

Other customs have evolved from that instinctive pride that vessels everywhere inspire in good masters. Those which have proved their worth for centuries may be slow to change. The proud Phoenician captain, watching lubberly maneuvers on a nearby craft, quite like a yachtsman of today, spat out: "Your ship is not well manned, your mariners are muleteers." And in *The Winter's Tale* a disgusted captain tells off a neophyte:

> Your moves were not in proper order.
> You had much ado to make [your] anchor hold;
> When you cast out, it still came home.
> With us at sea, we are strong in custom.

The various customs of saluting demonstrate goodwill and also render honors. As we know, the hand salute, although never rendered when the head was uncovered, removed the hand from side arms, and gun salutes unloaded cannon. Thus when John Paul Jones sailed his new American fleet into the harbor of Brest, France, he gave that port what seemed to him an inspired new idea: a fine salute of thirteen guns, the new United States of America being a thirteen-state nation, every shot being most carefully counted and timed by the sing-song phrase: "If I were not a gunner, I would not be here." The French, also counting every shot for number and for possible imperfect timing, thought it over and replied with nine guns, an equally inspired gesture doubtless considered as a becoming condescension from a monarchy to a mere democracy.

Of course, the practice of these subtleties evolved and varied with different ships and nations until now with widespread pleasure boating and a thousand different clubs, the game is being played too frequently without the needed rules that give it zest.

There was a saying: "Different ships, different long splices," which shrugged off the former minor differences quite well. But with the total change of scene today, even the best of modern skippers might well ask: "What in the world is a long splice?" The more studious may have seen a long splice pictured in old books on fancy knots and ropework, but its use has long since disappeared along with natural fiber cordage on boats.

Books and manuals of yacht routine, like the etiquette still spelled out in some club bylaws, call up many grand old customs regardless of the fact that their practice has disappeared along with the old types of props and equipment that made them possible. A good example is the changing sort of greetings exchanged by passing ships. In square-rig days the sailors, after being told to clean themselves, manned the rigging head to toe, arms outstretched, and gave three cheers as the ships swept by each other in all their majesty. As recounted in *The Merchant of Venice:*

> There, where your argosies with portly sail,
> Like signiors and rich burghers on the flood,
> Or, as it were, the pageants of the sea,
> Do overpeer the petty traffickers,
> That curt'sy to them, do them reverence,
> As they fly by them with their woven wings.

Then came steam. The yards and ratlines disappeared, and the customary greeting took on the formal navy regulation of saluting with an ensign-dipping flourish. Soon came the liners with their basso-profundo whistles that shook one's spine. Today we give a friendly wave or perhaps a hearty blast on our expensive air horn, and thus another custom has become established. A few purists are warning that it's all very bad form and could even be dangerous. They also sniff that whistling at another boat is as gauche as whistling at girls; that either one can cause trouble. Their objections may have some futile validity since certain whistle signals are prescribed by law to indicate steering intentions. The answer has to be that it's really not that difficult to distinguish happy tooling while passing from a prolonged one- or two-blast steering signal rendered far in advance of the passing. Anyway, the custom is here.

Yacht Club Tradition

It was undoubtedly that most dignified of clubs, the Royal Yacht Club of Cork, founded in 1720, whose routine and punctilio codified not only the rules of conduct for the proper yachtsman, but also the cast and mold of his thinking. The written rules defined his behavior and his dress. Example dictated his attitude, which was wholly that of the aristocracy. Wealth indeed was necessary, but the heraldic devices on his shield were even more important. In the mode of this brilliant example, there soon followed in the colonies other royal clubs, the Bermudan, in Bermuda, the Canadian in Toronto, and the Halifax in Nova Scotia.

And so it followed naturally that the New York Yacht Club, founded in 1848, followed at least the spirit, if not the noble titles, in their own yacht routine and their general outlook. However, being in a democracy, the club adopted some changes more in keeping with the realities of the New World. Following the Royal Cork example was not always possible nor appropriate.

It happened that the Race Committee of the Royal Yacht Club had been faced with an unusual protest. It seems that the yacht *Lulworth*, owned by a Mr. Joseph Weld, had been fouled at the weather mark by *Louisa*, owned by young Lord Belfast, while they were racing on a Sunday afternoon. It was claimed that *Louisa*'s crew swarmed aboard the *Lulworth* with drawn cutlasses and hacked down the running rigging and the steering gear. It was to this overly extrovert behavior by the bloody afterguard of rascals bearing noble titles that Mr. Weld objected.

After due deliberation the committee ruled in favor of *Louisa* and her sabre-wielding afterguard on the grounds that *Lulworth* represented only a tradesman, a tycoon to be sure but still a commoner.

Joe Weld, of course, knew the score, but he was sufficiently disgusted to show his contempt by building a beautiful steam yacht from whose quarterdeck he could survey with indifference the whole club fleet of sail, the owners of which did not seem to appreciate being looked down upon from a loftier deck.

While soiling one's hands in trade was considered as partially forgivable, the soiling of yachts with coal was viewed as total degradation. Therefore, *Lulworth* and her tainted owner were forever stricken from the roster.

Quite obviously, although New York lacked authentic titles among its membership, it did have plenty of the all-important scions of great wealth. In the fine tradition of its spiritual mother club in Cork, the nagging question of social acceptability of power in a yacht had so far not been fully considered, and all of their enrolled yachts had fitted easily in their assigned classes: those over sixty feet were Class I; the forty to sixty footers were Class II; and the small fry, the dregs, were acceptable as Class III. Power yachts were not mentioned until the secretary asked about J. P. Morgan's *Corsair*. She already flew the club burgee and had proved to be most commodious when hosting the race committee. The problem of sail versus power status will probably never be ironed out, but New York tried. Steam yachts were assigned to a new Class IV toleration. However, no sooner had this hydra head been tied down than another one arose across the sea and revealed the growing power of machinery afloat. An unexpected royal warrant suddenly gave status to the persistent engine-driven question. From the palace came this warrant to the Royal Yacht Club's secretary:

> Sir:
>
> I have it in command from His Majesty to acquaint you, for the information of the Commodore and Officers of the Royal Yacht Club, that as a mark of His Majesty's approval of an institution of such national utility as steam yachts, it is His gracious wish and pleasure that these shall henceforth be known and styled as the "Royal Yacht Squadron," of which His Majesty is graciously pleased to consider Himself the head.
>
> Belfast

Although much attenuated upon reaching these shores, the shock wave caused New York and the other older clubs to expunge their outward signs of nautical discrimination. The Boston Yacht Club, a faithful follower of the proper protocol, founded the Boston Power Squadron, followed quickly by the Portland Yacht Club down east in Maine with Power Squadron Number Two, and so on all across the country with power squadrons openly dedicated to the education of the great unwashed whose tastes were for machinery.

25

Status? What is it, anyway? It still remains a fact of pleasure-boating life, a fact created by the very popularity of power, that motor skippers as a class must still earn respect as seamen by their individual performance.

The reasoning would seem to be that "as a class," most small powerboats are quite simple to handle; some even have steering wheels and controls much like automobiles, and any hotshot driver can jump in and shove off, complete with standard freeway habits. On the other hand, the skipper of a sailboat, even a pitiful little Turnabout, has to understand how sails and wind relate. He has to "know the ropes," an endless study, his skill or lack of it immediately, perhaps disastrously, apparent.

All this transfer of Old World traditions to the New was more or less automatic. The New York Yacht Club, being the oldest, set the standards for clubs more recently established. Bylaws, copied by rote from New York, long since forgotten and ignored, either will not or cannot be complied with by the membership.

Yacht routine and etiquette become ever more useful and practical as the waterways become more crowded, but the niceties must merit general approval lest we find ourselves with no proprieties at all, only chaos, a situation rather unbecoming in a sport as deeply rooted as is our urge to get afloat and join with others of similar good taste. For example, in a section headed "Boats" many clubs prescribe the navy regulation that:

> Upon entering and leaving boats, deference is shown
> seniors, by juniors entering first and leaving last.

In no way does this fine old bit of navy apple-polishing refer to ladies or children, nor the mixed comings and goings of the club launch. It is strictly male, military, and misogynist.

Perhaps these bylaws should be examined. And while that study is in progress, it might be well to look at some other rules concerning boats. "Boats," in the old sense of transportation propelled by white-clad oarsmen, would seem to have given way to prams and dinghies and assorted outboards. But right there in the current yearbook it still states flatly that these boats shall display the flag of any club officer on board and that his juniors shall show him proper deference. Perhaps all references to boats are now quite academic anyway with so many clubs and marinas providing step-aboard convenience at permanent, plug-in berths.

Rank should indeed be accorded recognition, but that indication of respect had better fit with the facts of contemporary surroundings. We may be excused for marveling at the formal stiffness of a cocktail party aboard some grandly furnished 1890 yacht with the one-and-only head that served the owner's quarters. Such details have not been recorded, but undoubtedly the special deference accorded to the commodore by mere slobs, waiting their turn, preserved a great deal of important dignity.

Yacht Squadrons, so-called in all the old yearbooks, now vary widely in their facilities, but within the framework of contemporary life, agreeable amenities and their uses seem to be quite well understood without detailed explanations. It is the artificial etiquette which has become outmoded, not good manners.

Some Definitions

What were once important and humorless formalities have pretty much succumbed to present-day casual dress and actions. Since ninety-nine percent of all watercraft are now run and handled by their owners, once a small minority of self-styled "Corinthians," so-called in honor of their daring and luxurious sport, the dictionary definition of a yacht, as any boat sailed for pleasure, has fallen out of favor. We speak instead of boats, sailboats, cruisers, or outboards. For more exactness in these days of mass production, we may even name the makes. Those who really know go further and name the rig or class—a ketch, an Ensign, a trawler, a motor sailer.

As defined today by clubs that follow New York Yacht Club rules, enrollment in their yacht squadron is reserved exclusively for "those sailing vessels of twenty-five feet or more on the waterline, and motor craft of at least thirty-five on the loadline." In addition, to be enrolled as a yacht, either sail or power, "she must be designed, constructed, and equipped to be well able to accompany the Squadron on a cruise along the Atlantic seaboard and be fully decked, reasonable cockpit excepted."

These bylaws do not define "yachtsman," but the dictionary's definition is "anyone who sails for pleasure." That makes Cleopatra a yachtsman as well as that professional hell-raiser, Sir Francis Drake. He certainly sailed for pleasure. However, with pleasure boating now being indulged by the millions, the yachtsman and his yacht are spoken of in more familiar terms—skipper, sailor, boatman. The increasing common use of *boater* by newcomers has, with passing time, now dulled its jarring impact on more discriminating ears. A virtue of the English language is the ease with which new words and meanings enrich its power, but the line between enrichment and dead giveaway to ignorance can sometimes be very subtle. As Hilaire Belloc said: "A ship is a little world and she has a language of her own which disdains the land and its reasons."

The total terminology of all things nautical was vast and varied, far too esoteric for modern needs. Most of it is obsolete, but the few remaining terms fall easily on ears perceptive to the basic passwords. Perhaps there is no better explanation for the words that still survive except that they belong. Other old seagoing terms have long since become mere affectations, good buffoonery. To the brotherhood there is no *bow deck* nor *back of the boat* nor *prow.* There is the *forward deck* and the *afterdeck* or *stern* or *transom.* Even the still-heard *fantail* has not been a stern configuration for over half a century. But *leeward* is still pronounced *looward,* and most ropes on board are *lines* or anchor *rodes.* The skipper does not *drive,* he *takes the helm* unless he hands over that chore to someone else, and then he *conns* the ship. The line secured to a dinghy's bow is called a *painter* simply for the same reason that many other nautical terms have survived: it is short, specific, and understandable without mistake. A boat *casts off* or *shoves off* or is hoisted up on *davits,* correctly pronounced *dayvits* from the original David. Cargo and equipment are *stowed,* and a *well found* craft has specially fitted *stowage* space for every item of her *outfit.* Consumables are *stores* although they, too, are *stowed* away.

On salt water the speed is stated in *knots,* one knot being one nautical mile per hour, not a distance. To say, as do too many radio announcers, "ten knots per hour" indicates an acceleration of ten more knots every hour. Nautical charts of saltwater areas are scaled with one sea mile equaling one minute of arc of the earth's circumference. Charts of freshwater areas are scaled in land miles, and boat speeds are then in miles per hour.

Old-timers measured speed through the water by counting the number of knots on an accurately spaced chip log line that ran out over the stern while the sands of a twenty-eight-second glass ran down—hence, the term knots.

Stinkpotter and *ragman* are the mutually exclusive epithets hurled freely by the two great schools of boating folk, but these traditional opponents share a common disapproval of the overpowered speedboats which infest the waterways like fleas. By agreement, these wake-throwing nuisances have no resemblance to a yacht and their drivers' ancestors were something other than yachtsmen. Speedboats, whatever their size have their place, but that place is not in mooring areas nor busy waterways.

During times of truce we speak of *power skippers* and *sailors* though the self-styled sailors cherish noisy diesels

down below their fine teak hatches, and many a powerboat is skippered with good and proper handling. By the
same token it is interesting that many a smug sailor never
sails beyond the safety of the well-buoyed, afternoon race
course, while his counterpart in power may achieve his
most awesome cruises in high-speed dashes from one
plug-in marina to another one across the bay.

A great majority of boats today are small fry, especially the smaller outboards used mainly for Sunday fishing trips. Their owners and their pals or families may not
have much interest in boats as such or seamanship either
except as these things contribute directly to their fishing.
Fishing is their thing, not the magic of a boat's performance in great waters. If they find good fishing in charted
channels or tie their boats to Coast Guard buoys, we
should indeed point out that these are habits only of the
novice, and we may then suggest a safer way. But should
they have to learn by first capsizing in the swamping wake
of some larger craft laying its proper course by these
marks, we are ready to assist in rescue operations. Perhaps they will learn by our example, and we will have
done our part to foster another boating expert. Politeness, not profanity, should be our motto.

In passing we are led to wonder how the term "swear-
ing like a sailor" ever came about. Profanity has never
been exclusive to the sea; its language has always been
endowed with ample riches of its own. An interesting
early naval regulation warned the officers: "You shall
take especial care that God be not blasphemed in your
ship, but that after admonition be given, if the offenders

do not reform themselves, you shall cause them of the meaner sort to be ducked at the yardarm, and those of the better sort to be fined."

CHAPTER TWO

RULES OF THE ROAD

THE greatest single contribution to peace and harmony among nations, greater even than all the summit conferences combined, has been the universal acceptance of the nautical rules that govern rights of way.

Rules of the Road, codified today in the International Regulations for Preventing Collisions at Sea (COLREGS), doubtless had their origin in the dim, early history of Phoenician commerce and have been practiced ever since by sailors everywhere. The rules have been effective in spite of inflated nationalistic egos for the basic reason that sailors dislike collisions. They learned the hard and sometimes fatal way that assuming the right of way by dint of rank or bullheadedness was a form of bad manners that jeopardized their chances of getting home.

It is interesting that rules of conduct at sea, born of necessity in an effort to reduce mayhem, have been proving ever since the priceless pleasure of good manners. Would that this attitude bred of the sea were more prevalent ashore.

It is impossible to legislate politeness. Lloyd's Lutine bell, salvaged from the disastrous collision of the steamer *Lutine,* before its retirement in favor of an electronic collision announcement system, tolled more than fifteen thousand times for ships that bumped. Many of these insurance cases were caused by stubborn disregard of the simple rules by the masters of one or more vessels—something that was not only illegal but very bad form.

To cover all aspects of the Rules of the Road and every situation they govern would take a chapter the size of this book. My purpose in including a portion of them is to show how they can bring orderly behavior to vessels great and small and provide an international mandate for politeness and good manners at sea.

Basic to the rules of right of way is the Danger Zone, the arc from dead ahead to two points abaft the starboard beam. Every skipper must keep clear of any other vessel appearing in that small arc of designated danger. The only exception to this rule is a sailing vessel *under sail alone* which appears in the Danger Zone; it has the right of way over every other motor or steam vessel in all situations except when overtaking another vessel. The amazing beauty of this rule is that our own first responsibility is only 67.5 degrees, less than a third of the 360-degree horizon. The entire remainder, more than two thirds, is the other skipper's concern. What could be easier than that? Therefore, from directly ahead and around to about as far as the outstretched right arm can be comfortably swung requires constant watch because every boat within that arc has the legal right of way. However, let's

not act too much like lawyers: if some much larger or less maneuverable thing is coming at us from any other quarter, let's not stand on legality, righteously demanding our right of way. The reality is that, when all is said and done, the one universal illegality is the totally impersonal and revolting act of collision. Maritime law forbids indulgence in collision.

Therefore, when the larger craft is bearing down on us, whether a tanker, a ferry, or a tug towing barges, for example, and we have the right of way, we should be courteous and thoughtful of the other skipper's predicament. Nine times out of ten it is far easier for us to alter course and speed to avoid collision than for him. The important point in this situation is to make alterations decisively and early on so that the approaching vessel will understand our action. (There is nothing so baffling as dealing with another craft that does not know its own mind.) But never wait until sea room shrinks to nothing, lest we leave to our executor to explain that we had the legal right of way.

The usual situation in every busy harbor is the mixed coming and going of all types of craft—sail, power, fishing boats, and big commercial stuff. We can marvel that the multiangled, closely woven wakes do not result in devastation. But if we listen, we hear frequent, one-blast whistle signals announcing that this craft, seeing a potential right of way situation for herself, intends to maintain course and speed. The one other skipper to whom this situation is also apparent promptly gives a one-blast acceptance, and steers clear. Of course, should either party see some danger, the four- or five-blast warning must be sounded for "hold everything until we sort this out."

Let's consider a hypothetical situation, adapted from an illustration in *Chapman*. We are aboard the power cruiser number eight shown in the middle of this much foreshortened view of a helmsman's nightmare. She and all seven of the other boats have been running in the fog and have laid their compass courses on the harbor entrance buoy. Suddenly the buoy and the other boats can be discerned, and all boats refine their steering accordingly.

Boats one and two quite obviously have right of way over us in number eight, and are therefore privileged. Should either one see an approaching possibility of collision, thus becoming a situation where rules apply, she must sound one blast, meaning, "I intend to hold this course and speed and therefore let you see my one-syllable port side. Do you agree?" If that assessment seems correct, we reply in kind with our own one blast. Even if we, number eight, disagree, and think we have plenty of room and speed to cross ahead, we are not expected to sound the cross signal of two blasts: "I have the speed and I intend to cross ahead and leave you looking at my starboard side." Not only would that be rather impolite, but the action wouldn't stand a chance in court. No, we accept the other skipper's decision. Should we *really* have good reason to object to that one-blast signal, we must sound the danger signal of four or more blasts which requires that everything stop for reassessment, a ridiculous situation which no skipper of any goodwill would initiate.

Boat three is too far aft to be in our danger zone and therefore we are *her* concern rather than the other way around. We will remain alert, however.

Boat four, directly astern, is rapidly overtaking us. With a restricted channel looming ahead in the fog, she would pass close aboard and must therefore signal for permission to pass and indicate on which side she intends to pass. Again, her one-blast signal says: "I intend to show you my port side. Do you agree?" If we think she can do it safely without crowding us unduly, we answer in kind. If not, we blast the danger signal. Boat four must now either desist for the time being or try two blasts to see if we like her two-syllable starboard side any better. We answer in kind or with the danger signal.

We are in boat five's danger zone, but she is coming up slowly and she is of no immediate concern to us.

Boat six may be under sail alone and therefore privileged. We cannot be sure, but to be safe we can easily alter course and go around her stern so that no occasion for the rules will apply. Later, when this new, safe course takes us closer and we discover that she was motoring all the time with the jib hung up just for the hell of it, all hands exercise their self-control.

Boat seven may indeed be well outside our danger zone but she's coming on too fast for running in the fog, especially in the vicinity of an important buoy, which may mean that she is either on automatic pilot with the helmsman down below for coffee, or perhaps it's a lobsterman who knows that yachtsmen can usually be bluffed into giving way before their beautiful mahogany trim gets

DANGER ZONE

We are aboard number eight—in the center, above. Our danger zone is indicated by the shaded area: from dead ahead to two points abaft our starboard beam. In this instance, boats one and two are within "that small arc of designated danger."

rearranged. True enough, but had there been sufficient space on this page to depict true distances, it would have been apparent that we still had ample sea room for maneuvering, where all is clear and no rule need apply.

At night, with only running lights or range lights to indicate the other boat's direction, take it easy, very easy. It sometimes helps to remember the old jingle:

> Green to green or red to red,
> All is well and go ahead.

Strange, is it not, that the steering wheel of every standard make of runabout is still placed on the starboard side? The makers claim it offers a better view of the danger zone, and yet, in their own happy advertising, the leering young man at the helm is solely concerned with the bikini-clad young lady seated to port. Long years ago when a similar rule applied to vehicles ashore, that is, the car coming from the right had the right of way, the makers discovered that drivers like to talk to passengers: they lumped both danger zones together and put the steering wheel to port to provide for simultaneous surveillance of the dangers both near and far.

Fortunately, the sharing of thrilling exploits on the waterways is much more easily avoided than are high jinks on the highways. All we skippers of old-school courtesy may be of good cheer: those close, "me first" games need never spoil our day provided we have kept some sea room. After all, only when the possibility of collision becomes apparent do the rules apply. Therefore, either skipper who doubts the courtesy or common sense of his adversary may choose not to test the rules.

Let us consider this amazing proof of how civility and safety go together: for a period now nearing two centuries there has never been a peacetime passenger fatality on Cunard Line ships. This unique record has been established by captains who were not always commanding the best equipment but who were required by home office policy to follow strictly the well-known rules of courtesy and prudence. During the great days of the old "Atlantic Ferry," Cunard hauled more passengers than all other lines combined, lines featuring many more spectacular ships—and spectacular accidents.

Sam Cunard gave his captains this standing order:

> There shall always be two officers on watch. Bear in mind that your presence in the social halls is secondary to your duty on the bridge where your courtesy and prudence will avoid invoking rules concerning right of way.

In other words, he emphasized politeness on the bridge, and, alone among his contemporaries, he demanded absolute compliance with this and his other rules. Elsewhere the tendency has always been the attitude which favors celerity over civility. These rules, written in the days before black boxes, still speak clearly to the boating public of today:

> (1) Your own practical knowledge may be your best guide. (Mark Twain remarked that Cunard wouldn't hire even Noah without ten more years of training.)

(2) You shall respect your danger zone.

(3) Be civil to your passengers but recollect that they will value your services on deck . . . more than talking with them in the saloons.

(4) Never omit to verify your position by soundings. (Let today's skipper remember Lindsay's Law:
> "When your draft exceeds the water's depth
> You are most assuredly aground.")

(5) When overtaken by thick weather, you are not to be actuated by desire to complete the voyage on schedule; your sole consideration being the safety of your ship. (This policy was unique to Cunard captains.)

CHAPTER THREE

FLAGS AFLOAT AND ASHORE

> *He who would keep himself busy let him equip*
> *these two: a ship and a woman. For no two*
> *things involve more business once you start to*
> *fit them out, nor are these two ever sufficiently*
> *adorned, nor is any excess of adornment*
> *enough for them.*
>
> —*Plautus*

THAT anguished cry came straight from a yachtsman's soul. Plautus may have been a lesser scribe among the Roman playwrights, but he sensed the touching frustration known down the ages to every man who loves his boat. He probably would have drowned himself had he been faced with the equipment lists we struggle with today. On the other hand, they had more flags and bunting than we do now. They were part of that "excess of adornment" he wept about. Any craft without her colors has always been a tramp, probably a pirate. And to this day we feel there must be something furtive if a skipper sails without his colors. Perhaps he's just a neophyte who hasn't yet developed the pride in his vessel felt by good masters everywhere.

What other man-made object comes even near to more than twenty centuries of continuous affection? The Viking chief was buried with his ship. Clipper captains wagered fortunes on their beloved vessels. Yachtsmen, like many an addict, frequently ignore their budget limitations. The cause of this unique relationship may, as anthropologists have claimed, be some primal memory of man's own beginnings in the sea. But indeed the feeling does exist, and who needs further explanation as to why a boat is "she"?

Yachts display their colors for everyone to recognize—cruising boats, sport fishermen, race contestants, and even little runabouts. No boat's performance goes unnoted, for by her colors she represents a fleet with honored standards. Her actions constantly reflect the quality of those credentials that she holds in trust. On her day-in, day-out manners depends the reputation of her club and her skipper. The eyes of fellow yachtsmen are forever on her as a good or not-so-good example of the standards which her flags proclaim. To cast off and go without his colors is the privilege of the novice skipper, but by this omission he proclaims his status.

Flag adornments do lend a festive air, but more importantly at sea they indicate identity. The whole fore courses of Prince Henry's ships that fought their way around the tip of Africa were emblazoned with the cross of a wealthy order of the church. Columbus sailed with similar devices copied from the arms of Isabella and, if we

believe the etchings found on ancient vases, flags and bunting streamed from every stick and peak that would hold a halyard.

Three Marks of Identity

Down through the ages there have been three essential marks of identity for ships. Regardless of how many other flags and streamers she chose to fly, a vessel always indicated: 1. her country (the ensign); 2. her fleet (the burgee); and 3. her master (the private signal), in that order. The second club flag and ornamental whimsies follow. This is their order of importance in the boating scene. All that is necessary for absolute correctness, regardless of the boat's rig, is to start according to importance, matching flags to available positions. Where positions for the lower orders do not exist, then the lesser flags are just not flown, to state the obvious. However, only toy sailboats which never venture out beyond the harbor are exempt from flying any flags at all.

Designation of the stern as number one position for the country's flag was well established by the Roman custom of providing space for the VIPs along with little statues of their gods (called pupae) on the after deck— hence poop deck. In this area, drier and more favored than elsewhere aboard, the stench and filth of slaves were disguised with incense. In general, position number one, the place of honor, is still accepted as the area aft of midships. It may be either a staff at the stern or the peak of the aftermost gaff. Position number two is at the bow on powerboats or the foremost masthead on sailboats. Number three is at the signal masthead on powerboats or the second mast aft on sailboats. Number four is the main starboard spreader on any boat with a mast, and number five is a port spreader. Flag number one, the mark of nationality, goes in position number one. The club burgee, being next in line, goes in number two position. If there is no club affiliation flag to fill that spot, the private signal is moved up from number three to keep the number two position filled. With flags at just these two positions, runabouts and small fry are fully clothed, and larger craft are dressed, if not for company, at least for home waters.

On any boat, either sail or power, where the important masthead position has been obstructed by necessary instruments for navigation or racing, the simplest and best expedient is to upgrade all subsequent positions by one grade. That is, for sailboats the traditional number three position, the mizzen masthead on yawls and ketches, or the starboard spreader on sloops and ketches (as well as motor craft), becomes the designated number two position. Thus the burgee, second in importance only to the ensign, still displays its message of identity.

The Ensign

When fore-and-aft sail produced long, overhanging booms, the flagstaff on the taffrail had to go. While the poop deck area still retained its sanctity (although English navy dignity renamed it quarterdeck), the ensign stayed aft but was elevated to the afterpeak while under way.

This afterpeak is therefore position number one A. Quite rightly, custom bowed to convenience while under way, but it still shifted back to the stern staff when the hook went down. Until recently these two alternate positions served with equal honors, but with the advent of high aspect ratio sails on sloops and cutters, the backstay has appeared, and a flag flying from the leech (where custom placed an imaginary gaff) became most awkward, if not impossible. But since such rigs have short booms ending inboard, position number one still remains available and should be used both while under way and at anchor.

On powerboats, the skipper conns from somewhere forward of the stern where visibility is better. Guests and crew may be enthroned on a flying bridge or sheltered in a cabin. The after cockpit area while under way has lost its charm, what with no view forward and exhaust fumes tumbling in astern. Therefore, powerboats with signal masts took the hint from sailboats, installed a little gaff, and thereby had themselves a "peak," a place of honor with ready-made tradition. And, quite naturally, these innovative powerboats have introduced another new development. Not being handicapped with a gaff that lowers with the sail, they have no need to bother with restoring the ensign to the stern while at anchor. To leave the ensign thus flying high makes good sense. Loungers anywhere can take their ease while the ensign flaps contentedly well above their line of vision and undesecrated by boarding platform traffic. It is therefore obvious that positions one and one A share equal honors for every circumstance, and the choice depends entirely on which

one is the more convenient and better suited to the rig. With this option for all boats not racing, any failure to display an ensign is regrettable.

The flag to be flown from either of these honored number one positions depends, of course, on the vessel's registry. The United States, although having but one flag with legal status, widely recognizes the cherished custom of flying the so-called yacht ensign, the Betsy Ross flag with a fouled anchor within the circle of thirteen stars in the union. This flag, devised in 1847 by the New York Yacht Club as a signal to distinguish documented yachts, exempted them from commercial-type formalities of customs. It is also regarded as the one official ensign in the bylaws of that club as well as in the customary practice of most other American clubs and yachtsmen. It has a distinctively nautical appeal, and its overwhelming acceptance gives its use nearly the same sanction as formal law. The yacht ensign, therefore, flown by pleasure craft in American waters, has definitely become the maritime counterpart of the fifty-star national flag.

Strange, is it not, that the sailor's nightmare, a fouled anchor, should be considered nautical? Does this perhaps reveal the yachtsman's pagan prayer to be spared from such untimely misery?

Now and then some time-honored custom is flouted by intent, just to be different. An example is the grand old *Victory Chimes,* the former three-masted schooner-queen of all the Maine coast windjammer fleet. She flies the Stars and Stripes from her mizzen truck. For years horror-stricken armchair yachtsmen wrote letters to the editors.

They fumed about tradition, they denounced and deplored. But perhaps an even older custom is what has saved the smiling captain from the righteous mobs: "The King can do no wrong." If his Queen appeared in non-reg raiment, ergo, said raiment was correct. However, a word of caution: that kind of unilateral privilege is reserved for royalty; on lesser craft it doesn't look the same.

Time of Colors

The yacht ensign is displayed between morning and evening "colors" from 0800 to sunset except on unmanned craft and in foul weather. The times may be taken from the senior officer present afloat, the yacht club cannon, or, if gunkholing alone, from one's own good judgment. The 0800 time is old navy custom, allowing ample daylight hours for the crew to swab down decks before the brass turns to. Sunset in a club anchorage is when the cannon bangs out official permission for the sun to call it a day, a time not to be confused with the armchair yachtsman's "over-the-yardarm" time for gin and tonic.

Although past custom has called for ensigns to be an inch or more on the fly for each foot of overall boat length or mast height, perhaps an inch or less would be more suitable today in view of the prevalent shorter staffs and less flamboyant flag displays.

The Burgee

Position number two, the bow staff on powerboats or the foremost truck on sailing craft, is for the flag of next importance, the burgee of fleet identity. For pleasure

52

craft, that would be a club or some other boating group. Burgees are usually triangular, sometimes swallowtail, three-eighths to half an inch on the fly per foot of boat length or mast height, whichever is greater. If the skipper has no club or group affiliation, this second most important flag position should be filled by flying his private signal there, as mentioned before and discussed in detail later. There should be no intermediate position gaps.

Summary of Yacht Flag Code

Name of Flag	Position
1. Ensign Either the fifty-star, U. S. national flag or the thirteen-star yacht signal	*Power:* Either the stern staff or peak of signal mast gaff *Sail:* Boats with the modern short boom may display the ensign either at stern staff or two-thirds up the backstay while under way or at anchor. Boats with overhanging boom use stern staff only while at anchor. Underway halyard is rigged from peak of aftermost gaff.
2. Burgee	*Power:* Bow staff *Sail:* Forward masthead or, if obstructed, main starboard spreader or after masthead
3. Private Signal or Officer Flag (if skipper is a flag officer of club shown by burgee)	*Power:* Signal masthead *Sail:* Starboard spreader if available. If not, port spreader or an after starboard spreader

4. Second Boating Organizations	*Power and Sail:* Starboard spreader. Preferred position for displaying the U. S. Power Squadrons ensign
5. Whimsical Flags	*Power:* Port spreader only *Sail:* Any otherwise vacant port spreader
6. Foreign Host	*Power and Sail:* Foreign host country flag takes precedence over all others at main starboard spreader.

Bow Staffs

Bow staffs on some mass production boats have been subjected by landlubber "product stylists" to indignities which render them all but useless. Bow staffs, signal masts, and even radio antennas are laid down at streamlined angles which are not only ugly but impair their usefulness and frequently create a vision-flapping nuisance. The owner of a boat equipped with these lubberly aberrations should make a winter project of putting things to rights.

Yachts are frequently enrolled in the squadrons of more than one club or boating group. In the absence of specific bylaws, we simply let courtesy and convenience be the guide as to which burgee to fly. Ordinarily, only the home club or group burgee will be displayed. However, when visiting one's other club or when cruising with any other fleet in which the yacht is enrolled, it is most appropriate to be identified as a member of that fleet. It has been the stated custom to replace a hometown burgee

55

with that of the immediate fleet—sometimes quite a nuisance. Perhaps a better way on some occasions would be to fly the burgee of the moment at number four position if the hoist at that position is available, thereby eliminating much shifting about.

Union Jack

The so-called Union Jack, a square blue flag with fifty stars, has no identity significance at all. Of strictly naval origin, its only function as flown from a special jackstaff appears to be a statement that this vessel with more than one mast is at anchor in sunny weather and that the day is Sunday or some sort of a holiday. Today, the average sober yachtsman with a little help from his first mate can estimate the truth of those details almost at a glance, even without the Union Jack. As merely decorative bunting, a Union Jack or two could be useful among the other pretty flags in a dress-ship hoist or, just for the fun of it, flown from the otherwise empty port spreader.

The Private Signal or Officer's Flag

"The owner of every yacht entitled to fly the Club Burgee shall have a private signal." So reads the bylaw of the New York Yacht Club. This requirement to have a private signal is also stated by many other clubs, and their designs are published in the yearbooks. Less formal clubs urge or encourage private signals. Few members really know their club's official stand, but there is no question as to the signal's propriety and enjoyment. The private signal is displayed from position number three: the truck of the signal mast on powerboats or the mizzen masthead on yawls, ketches, and schooners; or starboard spreader on sloops and cutters. This position is the third in importance and is reserved for the third detail of identity except for facilities of the Coast Guard Auxiliary whose regulations are outlined later. If there is no third position and if there is no club affiliation, a private signal should be moved up to number two position.

Like a sailboat mast, the powerboat's signal mast may be vertical or slightly raked, at most not more than ten degrees. More rake than this is a misguided distortion of marine requirements. The signal mast should be tall enough to spread its yardarms well above the head of anyone standing on the topmost deck. Its flags and halyards should not be in the helmsman's line of vision. Such a mast can add to the height and efficiency of radio antennas and will keep lights and flags out of the way. A vertical whip antenna, in the absence of a regular signal mast, offers a reasonably good substitute for the signal mast's position number three, provided the halyard block lacks disturbing dielectric properties.

The private signal is designed as a strictly personal device, usually swallowtail and about the same size as the burgee. *Lloyd's Register of American Yachts,* before it ceased publication in 1978, listed and pictured over three thousand of these descendants of heraldry. The motif, or device, should be simple for easy recognition and, if possible, symbolic of the owner—a hallmark, if you will. Sticklers for purity frown on using letters or initials, but certainly any block letters which read the same from either side should be considered just as appropriate as any other pictographs. The eleven block letters, A, H, I, M, O, T, U, V, W, X, and Y, are therefore suitable if your initial is one of these. They create a bold design with the same silhouette on either side, avoiding the double-exposure effect which clutters the mainsail on many "class" sailboats.

A flag officer of any club or group whose burgee is being displayed at the time will, of course, fly the flag of office in place of a private signal. Bylaws of most clubs state that officers' flags shall be displayed both day and night in the place and instead of any private signal, or in the case of a single-masted sailboat, instead of the burgee, except when racing. This impractical day and night requirement for flags of office (also for the Cruising Club of America burgee), if followed, means seven twenty-four-hour days a week, which will very shortly reduce the flag to tatters. No doubt this lofty egotism was inspired by the rank-happy officer who first sewed stripes on his pajama sleeves. If the club will foot the bill for a dozen flags for every officer, the custom might be revived. Otherwise, the normal skipper displays the colors only when on board, between 0800 and sunset and when it isn't blowing half a gale.

Coast Guard Auxiliary Flag Code

A privately owned boat under the command of a Coast Guard Auxiliarist displays her colors as prescribed by the United States Coast Guard which, like the Navy, is a

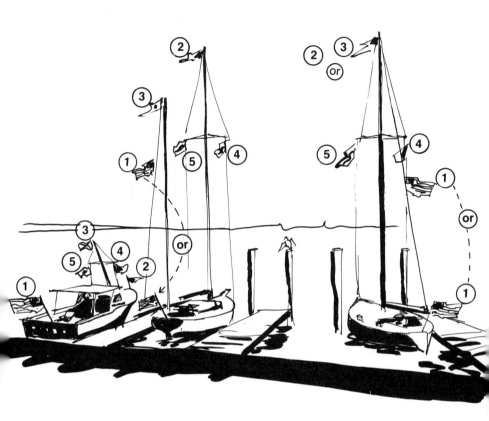

1. The ensign
2. The burgee
3. The private signal
4. The second club
5. Ornamental whimsy

direct arm of government. Therefore, the Auxiliary quite rightly flies the only legal national flag: the fifty-star ensign rather than the popular yachty substitute, the thirteen-star New York Yacht Club signal.

The major variation in the relative status or pecking order between the Auxiliary and the general yacht routine occurs in the switched priorities of masthead and bow staff. The Auxiliary claims the masthead for its number two position, displaying its own ensign at that hoist— that is, the truck, or if the mast, at least clipped up somehow on the radio antenna. If neither of these positions exists, the bow staff will have to serve, but only as a temporary expedient. Other than this exchange between bow staff and masthead, the relative position status of Auxiliary and general routine are quite similar. The next position for identification is the same for either, the bow staff.

Next in line is, of course, the individual flag. If the skipper is a flag officer of the group indicated by the burgee at the bow, the flag of that office flies from the starboard spreader. If the skipper is neither currently a flag officer nor a flagged past officer, a private or personally designed flag reflects the assurance expected of a good officer and skipper.

In cases of dual membership, such as U. S. Coast Guard Auxiliary and U. S. Power Squadrons, or perhaps two yacht clubs, the flag of the one least concerned with activities of the moment adds a bit of color on festive occasions. However, cocktail flags or any other such trivia are quite beneath the dignity of the Auxiliary.

Status Bunting

Position numbers four and five are essentially the same for either sail or power and offer some pleasant ways to proclaim any lesser details. Number four is usually the starboard spreader on power craft; the main spreader on sailboats if there is more than one mast. This position is for the second club burgee or, as is still graven in too many books, messages pertaining to owner or the guests. Number five is the foremost spreader on the port side. According to the still-printed bylaws, this one announces doings of the crew, at one time in yachting history when that group of worthies was a very numerous and hungry contingent. It would now seem that priority at this position is the place for surplus colors only.

Gala Flags

To the credit of the sport, there are some rare occasion flags in the well-stocked wardrobe for a lady's full adornment. On regatta days, for parades and special holidays, "dressing ship" is quite in order, but not exactly in the old and time-honored manner. Profoundly stated in the older books:

> On the Fourth of July and when ordered on other occasions, a yacht in commission shall, when at anchor and the weather permits, dress ship from morning to evening colors. Rectangular flags should alternate with pennants. Ensigns, burgees, private signals, and officer flags shall

not be included among code flags and pennants in the hoist in dressing ship.

Also, it was required that this hoist extend from the waterline forward, up to the stemhead, thence over the truck, down to the taffrail, and drop to the waterline aft.

Although the United States Yacht Racing Union and other racing and crusing associations still print the requirement that offshore yachts shall carry code flags, their usefulness has long since vanished, and the rule is generally ignored. The fact is that code flag communication among yachts is but a memory, and code flags, if aboard at all, remain to mildew in the locker. Even the specified "T" flag (for transportation) is unhappily ignored by the club's own launch. Since World War II the launch has answered only to whistle signals (*horn* in modern parlance) or to VHF-FM calls.

Already well established is the custom of creating dress ship hoists out of any surplus bunting and miscellany that every boat accumulates, plus a couple of dozen pennants liberated from some friendly used car lot. A parade or anchorage looks festive in direct proportion to the brightness of the colors and the numbers of those who display dress ship makings, whatever the happy bunting may be. Actually, this new casualness is still somewhat in line with the old bylaw since those motley flags will definitely not be "among code flags" in the hoist. The modern way also eliminates those soggy tailenders trailing to the waterline. The hoist can be made up with each flag on a tack line fitted with a toggle and an eye splice, allowing each flag to be readily removed or changed; or, the flags can be spaced along a single line tailored to the ship, with each flag sewed to the line.

Fleet Captain's Flag

Although fleet captains, for some forgotten reason, have been restrained from any display of their flag of office "except while performing their official duties in a small boat," whatever that may mean, they are obviously flag officers by virtue of the simple fact that they have a designated flag, exactly like the rear commodore's flag but without the circle of stars. Since his duties include whatever the commodore designates, they are no more nebulous than those of the rear commodore and he (or she) certainly should fly that flag of office whatever the size of the boat, at least from that formerly crew-designated port spreader or, still better, from the masthead, like any other officer.

Like the fleet captain, the chaplain and fleet surgeon are usually appointed rather than elected, but since the latter two offices have generally gone out of fashion, their flags need not be considered.

For ordinary members with no claim to any office and for past officers who have served their terms, we let them fly a designated past officer's flag or any pretty bunting from position number five if they crave more color. Perhaps that lonesome port-hand position should also be revived for containment of the so-called "fun" flags.

Half-Masting

As specified in the yacht routine of the New York Yacht Club, the United States Yacht Racing Union, and in general acceptance, ensigns (the national flag) are half-masted only on occasions of national mourning. The bylaw reads as follows:

> On Memorial Day the ensign is half-masted from 0800 to 1200. On the death of a yacht owner, the club burgee and his private signal may be half-masted on his yacht. When the Yacht Club orders mourning for the death of a member, other members' yachts at anchor, the clubhouse, and stations shall half-mast the burgee only. Flags shall first be mastheaded and then lowered one third.

Half-masting is certainly a beautiful and respectful custom, but it poses difficulties as to how it can possibly be accomplished on today's boats. As with dipping the ensign for salutes (discussed later in this chapter), physical realities of size of today's boat and its facilities, lack of on-board crew, and availability of owners preclude the ceremony. In general, then, watercraft must leave half-masting to the shoreside stations where flagpoles and halyards still exist. However, half-masting the burgee and the member's private signal, if he had one, from the club's flagpole certainly deserves consideration. The private signal, in this case, should be displayed from the port yardarm, or, if there is no yardarm, from the same halyard as the burgee and below it, both being hoisted to the truck at 0800 and promptly lowered about one-third of the height to the half-mast position. At 1200 they should be two blocked again, and the private signal only lowered and removed.

Some theorists have suggested that the Memorial Day time of 1200 for mastheading should be, say, 1215 to match the actual time at Arlington when the bugle call of Taps may have sounded its requiem. An interesting thought but then we might as well allow for zone time differences, too. Let's forget it.

Obsolete Flags

The present bylaws still provide for an "owner absent flag," a rectangular blue flag indicating that the owner is not on board at the moment. It is punctiliously displayed by naval vessels when the commanding officer steps ashore. It is hauled down smartly at the instant when this officer returns and sets foot on deck. However, what with assailing thieves more common today than pirates once were off a have-not nation's coast, a private owner would be wise to drop the whole idea and have his club's official flag routine revised.

A similar blue flag but with a diagonal white stripe is also provided for in traditional yacht routine. It signified that although the owner is absent, his wife or some guests are aboard and may have found the liquor locker. While its general import is also to signify that this boat may now be under charter to strangers, it has been known to indicate that the cat's away and the coast is clear. Or in the case of modern corporate ownership, one may wonder who really is the absentee. But, all things considered, perhaps a very well known private yacht when under charter might still, for personal convenience, display that flag.

Again, for position number four, the old but still prescribed routine mentions an "owner's meal flag," rectangular white, indicating that the owner is now being fed and may be dangerous if interrupted. First mates, take note: before you hand that poached egg on toast to your Lord and Master, clip a napkin to the halyards and hoist it to position number four. Your time could come when you raise a red pennant to position number five, meaning that the crew is now enjoying well-earned time out and wants no visitors. Not that anyone would understand these family pranks, but it's spelled out as gospel on many a musty page.

The owner absent and, of course, the crew's meal flag should be expunged. Position number five should be for what it has in fact become: the overflow position for any non-reg bunting, past officer flag, or any pretty colors which the heart desires.

Lights

There is very little to be said about the lights which are still prescribed for proper designation of rank. Let's not belabor the dead. It is sufficient to point out that bylaws which prescribe two vertical blue lights on the commodore's flagship (red for vice commodore and white for rear commodore) are simply no longer observed. If another blue light is added to indicate owner absent, flag-ships could be quite attractive—to uninvited guests. More appropriate might be a strobe light wired to a burglar alarm.

Apparently there are no other lights remaining in the status category although the thirty-two-point mast-head light deserves some comment. This is the legal anchor light required except in designated small-craft harbors. In days of coal-oil lanterns, most skippers dutifully complied, nuisance though it was. The lanterns were forever blowing out or sooting up their chimneys or crashing down on deck. Today, even with electric light convenience, the anchor light is trustfully neglected in many nonofficial gunkholes in deference to the battery, and, of course, berthing at marinas eliminates the need for anchor lights. On the other hand, one frequently spots an early evening anchor light or two among the fleet off larger yacht clubs. This is probably a bit of pardonable one-upmanship. It innocently flaunts the surplus juice which this well-favored vessel has in such abundance.

Running lights and their arcs of visibility are speci-fied by law. The prudent skipper will avoid the common streamlined versions which appeal to neophytes but do not separate the color arcs. These toy lights fail in their single most important function: indicating the boat's di-rection. They are dangerous, illegal, and not even ornamental.

CHAPTER FOUR

SIGNALS, COMMUNICATIONS, AND SALUTES

"THERE'S something wrong with our bloody ships today," growled Vice-Admiral Sir David Beatty (as quoted in Winston Churchill's *World Crisis*) after having requested information by code flag and blinker light during the battle of Jutland. The reply, completely unexpected, promptly came from the German fleet in the form of devastating salvos from their sixteen-inch guns. That was probably the end of visual communications. Navies now resort to a few nostalgic training exercises with their mildewed code flags mainly as a test of secrecy, now practically assured by the present scarcity of old Boy Scouts.

Race committees have standardized their routine flag hoists, all well known and understood ahead of time. During races, yachts hoist the red code flag B to protest foul play. Distress is indicated by any means at all that will get attention, the most effective now being the telephone. Most clubs and marinas monitor the distress and working channels.

69

NAUTICAL ETIQUETTE AND CUSTOMS

All of which has brought about a whole new line of
mandated courtesies to be followed carefully or the FCC
(Federal Communications Commission) becomes quite
upset. To paraphrase Bobby Burns: "There's a monitor
among you takin' notes, and faith, he'll cite you."

Radiotelephones

Many of the rules for shipboard telephones keep changing as needs are demonstrated, but the basic principle of
courtesy remains. For example, it is mandatory that the
vessel's name and call sign precede and follow every
message. We want to know who's talking. Also, for our
safety, the designated channel must be monitored and
reserved exclusively for calling and distress, promptly
shifting to a message channel. Small craft using only CB
sets are liable to find their favorite channels swamped by
unknown gossipers and that's the major drawback to CB.
Sensible politeness plus vigilance by all true yachtsmen
can help to keep VHF-FM free of this nuisance. With the
advent of dual monitoring, clubs and marinas can further
reduce the traffic on the designated channel while still
listening for other calls.

Perhaps no other category of boating behavior is
more neglected than the careful use of telephones. The
neophyte forgets that he is on a party line of thousands;
the lonesome fisherman spins endless yarns about the
paucity of fish; the drunken sailor airs his limited vocabulary; all of these and more compound a misdemean-
or into maddening frustration when the abusers fail to

shift to working channels. The heedless talker may be cited by the FCC or, which is much more disgraceful, he may be ridiculed by fellow boatmen.

Calls for assistance are, of course, given full priority. We do not break in on conversations between a troubled boat and the Coast Guard unless real help can be offered. But whatever the signal of distress may be—waving of shirts, or shouts, or flashlight beams—we are obliged to investigate, stand by, and do a seaman's duty. For telephones, the FCC has given this protocol the force of law, a legislated politeness so needed in our present overcrowded air.

Fortunately, the new cellular telephone networks are gradually being constructed, the first ones being in the Gulf of Mexico. This is very similar to the cellular mobile networks already serving many major metropolitan areas on land. It will become a welcome system for smaller craft operating within a few hundred miles of shore. The name "cellular" derives from the grid of overlapping cells, each with a low-powered transmitter. These are linked to a central switching computer where calls are patched into the network. The system can handle thousands of calls simultaneously with direct-dialing privacy to any phone number in the world. Calls are "duplex"; that is, they provide the regular land-based type of listening and talking at the same time without switching. No operator's license is required.

Already in full service on several thousand ocean-going ships is the INMARSAT (International Maritime Satellite) system which gives global coverage except for polar regions. This system is somewhat more expensive, but it provides all the convenience of direct dialing to any telephone in the world, a boon to ship operators, cruise ship passengers, or deep sea fishermen who like to keep their business secrets secret.

The future of communications for most yachts and other small craft will apparently be in the cellular system, but in the meantime, the presently required forbearance continues to be the rule.

Dipping the Ensign

A typical section of yacht routine as presently set forth by old-line clubs is as follows:

> All salutes herein provided shall be made by dipping the ensign once, lowering the ensign to the dip, and hoisting when the salute is returned. All salutes shall be returned.
>
> (a) Vessels of the United States and foreign navies shall be saluted.
>
> (b) When a yacht in which a flag officer is embarked comes to anchor, all yachts shall salute, except when there is a senior officer present.
>
> (c) When a yacht comes to anchor where a flag officer is present, such flag officer shall be saluted.
>
> (d) A junior officer anchoring in the presence of a senior shall salute, and the salute shall be returned by the senior flag officer only.
>
> (e) Yachts passing shall salute, the junior saluting first.
>
> (f) On yachts displaying no ensign or displaying an ensign which cannot be dipped by the use of halyards,

the captain renders and returns salutes by a hand salute or by doffing cap or hat.

(g) All salutes shall be returned in kind.

After careful reading of that explicit protocol, and pondering the busy boating scene today, we marvel at the beauties of that era—that formal, uncrowded era, when there was time and room in which to live. There was joy in opulence, there was pride and privilege in making a ceremony of politeness. But as of now the only small reminders of that grand routine are those moldering words, unheeded by a generation far too busy making bigger waves or just tending sheets without paid hands. Yet, wayward and unsanctioned though they be, new customs have evolved which need only to be codified.

As has been pointed out, the vast majority of yachts today could not dip the ensign even if they would. And those few which could should not because, according to the foregoing paragraph (g), salutes shall be returned in kind unless, paragraph (f), the senior captain, probably indifferent to his seniority, is embarrassed into rendering a hand salute or doffing his cap. With modern flagstaffs not much higher than their hoists, to say nothing of their pristine lack of halyards, perhaps the staff might be yanked from its socket for enthusiastic waving of the stick, if indeed it could be reached at all while under way. But paragraph (f) about halyards seems to exclude that solution anyway. Civilian hand salutes are out of fashion, also. And how many years ago was the last flag officer saluted by all yachts when he came to anchor? Or by any single boat, junior or otherwise?

73

To quote further:

Guns may be used to call attention to signals, but their use otherwise shall be avoided as much as possible. Whistles shall never be used in saluting.

It would seem that when that proper dipping of the ensign was not duly answered, an insulted captain could resort to cannonading but never, never to whistling. So here again, the grand old ways have been forgotten and, by those few who have ever read their nostalgic yearbooks, forgiven, with understanding. The whole routine must be revised and, like politics, be settled for the possible.

Passing Salutes

The passing situation is among those great occasions which are listed as proper for saluting. Due perhaps to population growth, the passing salute has now in fact become an arm-wave greeting. It is universal. Some arm-chair types deplore it on the grounds that a frantic wave of desperation or distress might be mistaken for just another friendly greeting. It is reported that heedless neophytes have done just that, to boating's shame.

The ancient rule to stand by and give assistance to any vessel in distress has never been incorporated into bylaws, but it exists, just as the arm-wave greeting now exists in quite satisfactory replacement of ensign-dipping, junior-senior games.

Horn tooting (the vernacular for whistle sounding), as mentioned in Chapter One, is another more or less unsanctioned form of greeting between passing boats. It can be quite acceptable provided it is given in a manner that is unmistakable as only a happy greeting. We should remember that the duties of the whistle (horn) include requests for bridge openings, launch service, danger warnings, and, very importantly, steering intentions. These are vitally essential safety regulations and should not be subject to possible confusion. For example, the steering-intent signal of one prolonged blast means: "we intend to show you our one-syllable port side; do you agree?" Likewise two blasts means showing our two-syllable starboard side. Of course, that isn't the official wording but when remembered that way, it has certainly helped many a nervous skipper look good. Perhaps your greeting could conceivably be misinterpreted as an overly delayed steering signal if not delivered well ahead of time, but since greetings are delivered only during the actual passing (when obviously too late to indicate a proposed future action), it would seem that the custom as already existing might well be considered fully as acceptable as the arm wave is.

In regard to greetings and salutes involving cruising fleets and rendezvous, the old standard bylaw reads:

A yacht which has joined the squadron during the annual cruise shall request permission before leaving. When meeting squadrons of other clubs, salutes shall be exchanged by the senior officer present. When meeting a single yacht, the salute shall be answered only by the flagship.

This is another bylaw to be expunged entirely for reasons quite clear to any cruising yachtsman who has had the pleasure of being waved to, and waving back, to every craft nearby, singly or in a passing fleet. That a brand new senior officer may have polished off his by-the-book saluting would be regarded as a bit of happy clowning. No skipper can ignore a friendly wave although, quite naturally, some sailboat skippers have been known to keep both hands grimly occupied when some wake-throwing motor cruiser, frequently flagless, goes piling by. (The inadequate skipper bolsters his self-esteem with horsepower in lieu of horse sense; he is overly impressed with the greatness of his spectacle.)

The conclusion must be drawn that only on occasions of very special pageantry such as formal parades and commemorative ceremonies will the old salutes be rendered. But even here the practice must be fitted to the practical. This is how it should be because this is how it seems to work.

A yacht about to join a fleet at anchor nowadays announces her arrival by means of telephone on a designated channel. If it is intended to join a raft-up, there should be agreement as to port or starboard landing with fenders out accordingly. If anchoring or if there is a mooring or a slip, this is similarly discussed by telephone. After such advance announcements of arrival, all the greetings necessary are volunteered by zealous line handlers or in the form of the usual sage advice on how to anchor.

Boarding Other Boats

When visiting other boats, whether they be tied up at a float or moored out by themselves, the standard navy greeting *cum* request is always suitable: "Permission to come aboard, Sir?" The formal regulation answer is a noncommittal "Permission granted." With suitable inflection we can make that answer ring with pleasure.

Should a flag officer ask permission to come aboard, the old rule, still on the books, requires that if he is "senior to the yacht boarded, his flag shall be displayed at the starboard spreader while he is aboard." Otherwise "he should be considered as present only in an unofficial capacity."

Perhaps that delightful excess of formality could just be wiped off the books without bothering to cook up any replacement. By the time we might have determined the commodore's capacity, liquid or official, it would no longer matter that a commodore flag was not available anyway. Happily, most visiting is just "boat-hopping," and the visitor's obligations will be limited to the permission request and subsequent comments about something good in the boat. Every skipper wants his boat, like his dog, to be appreciated.

CHAPTER FIVE

CEREMONIES ASHORE AND AFLOAT

A LL of us enjoy ceremonies and panoply on great occasions. Back in the days when yachting was strictly a royal pastime, beginning with Cleopatra and carried on with gusto by England's King Charles II, Russia's Peter the Great, and the venerable clubs, the pageantry of military splendor and rank demanded full display, both afloat and in the clubhouse. In short, the flaunting of a private navy went hand in hand with the uninhibited enjoyment of wealth and high position.

Nautical etiquette today differs widely from the props and purposes so much a part of the old magnificence. It has shrunk to fit our democratic tastes. Chambers of Commerce and special committees, on the other hand, promote parades of any kind that will add color to their civic events, and frequently they turn out to be worthwhile affairs, even for the yachtsmen who participate.

Boat launchings, at least for custom craft, are still worthy of a celebration. Springtime club commissioning can be a most delightful exercise. The Change of Watch, when a new club slate takes over the bridge, merits an "occasion" as well as do trophy presentations and new member parties. A good program aims at somewhere between the indifferent and the ostentatious. The one can be an amateurish disappointment, the other a wearisome pomposity. Too much simplicity can leave out those pleasant moments where the individual may shine; excess formality is artificial in view of today's first-name basis common in all of our clubs. Quasi-naval uniforms have been pretty much outgrown by boating people. Blue blazers with a breast pocket patch featuring the club burgee serve quite well for all club functions.

Launching Parties

Most boats today, like automobiles, burst forth as finished products and first beguile their owners from a dealer's showroom. They are then deposited in the water by travelift or trailer. The owner signs the truckman's book and then shoves off to try his newest toy.

There's something missing here, something that could have been a lot of fun, the fun that seems to be remembered only for those craft of custom build. Not that custom building means more expensive or resplendent boats; not at all. It's simply that the stock boat buyer usually forgets to plan a party. It's a pity.

Somewhere along the line of hurried commerce, either while that boat is being grappled by a monster lift or loaded on a trailer, she should be made a member of the family. She should be christened. The photogenic high point of a christening is when the favored female

79

slams the bottle and sings out: "I christen thee *Naomi*," The beribboned champagne bottle (probably containing ginger ale) breaks with a satisfying crash and foaming spray. The gods will look with favor on this well-born craft, and friends are properly impressed.

First, there has to be a bottle. Ersatz champagne in precracked and decorated bottles is stocked in larger chandleries, but an ordinary soft drink bottle can be made to serve if the decorative covering is stout enough to confine the flying glass should the little lady be instructed to swing with real determination. Such bottles can be tough to break, but there's good tradition for prescoring the glass and for a hefty swing. It is written that the climax of a Viking christening party overwhelmed all evil spirits when the noble chieftain swung and broke the back of a robust well-bound prisoner across the vessel's stem. The splendor of that spurting blood transferred the hapless victim's strength to those graceful lines of innocent seakindliness. Beauty, full circle.

As refined in centuries of softening, the prepared-and-decorated bottle and the Little League approach will assure a foaming crash for good pictures and for the merry onlookers. For an added nicety, some bunting can be draped over the boat's name so that it can be snatched aside when the bottle smashes. Extending the party further at the launching site will depend upon facilities for exclusion of casual freeloaders. Custom boats launched from the builder's yard have no restriction but, whether stock or custom, big or small, a boat deserves a christening, and the owner deserves a party. Probably few festivi-

ties have deeper roots in widely varying traditions. Convenient changes in the format, therefore, will still propitiate some pagan god or other.

Club Commissioning

All yacht clubs in northern waters close down their boating seasons during winter months and then reopen in the spring with some sort of celebration. The larger clubs stage ceremonies built around a four-hoist flag-raising complete with blue blazers, white pants, salutes, and a band. Smaller clubs may just raise the flag. Most clubs go for something in between. Some clubs have a flagpole full rigged with yardarm and gaff; others have just the pole. There are at least some sixteen hundred clubs, all with differing facilities and circumstances, but the grand old spectacle of Joe Dokes civilians in "play navy" uniforms has, in compliance with the more sophisticated and casual approach suited to the sport, become less appropriate. Nevertheless, a loyal membership deserves to have this first flag raising of the season be of some importance, and therefore all the officers and chairmen should at least be dressed as nearly alike as possible.

A commissioning ceremony is the only occasion where colors are not made at 0800. They are made when the entertainment committee and the club officers decide to have the party, usually in the late afternoon when more members and guests can be present. The officers and chairmen should be lined up in ranks facing the flagpole and in full view of members. Junior yacht club officers may be assigned to attend halyards. Upon word from the commodore, the fleet captain, stationed where convenient, orders the steward to "fire when ready." The cadets then raise their respective halyards, the yacht ensign to the peak of the gaff, the club burgee to the truck, and the commodore's flag to the starboard yardarm, going up together but being careful to two block the ensign first. All hands, being uncovered, come to breast salute. The fleet captain turns to the commodore and reports: "Sir. The Seagull Yacht Club is now in commission for the 19-- season." The commodore replies with "Thank you, Captain," and turns to the spectators with: "At ease, ladies and gentlemen. I now present to you our officers and chairmen." Whereupon flag officers, the vice and rear commodores, step forward to be individually introduced while their flags of office are displayed at the port yardarm. The halyard handlers are instructed to lower the vice commodore's flag in time to prepare the hoist for prompt display of the next flag as the rear commodore steps forward. That flag is then lowered as introductions and duty descriptions of committee chairmen start. The commodore's flag, as always, remains at the starboard yardarm for as long as the commodore is on the clubhouse grounds or aboard his boat in the club anchorage.

It all takes a bit of planning to bring the show off smoothly. It may well require some enticing notes by a bugler to get ebullient members away from the bar and outside to see the show and be among those present when the official photographer is catching action for the yearbook.

Parades

In former, less crowded days, parades were much more easily arranged than in these times when busy owners plan ahead for every precious boating hour. A mere parade which happens to conflict with long-planned cruising or scheduled racing will get very low priority from possible participants today. But if the timing is fortuitous and the excuse a popular one, parades can be successful, even rewarding. They need a lot of staff work. They must be part of a more extensive program. That is, a parade must be more than just a spectacle for the shore bound "other half" if the boating people are to feel well compensated for their time. There must also be some subsequent attraction, a rendezvous or a banquet with the VIPs, or at least a well-catered picnic.

A good parade should be reviewed, and that requires a personage and a beautiful retinue to be saluted, all with some degree of order in the general enthusiasm. Politicians may be somewhat reluctant to appear so well regarded by the idle rich. Therefore, agreement on a personage may depend on fortuitous circumstances which have created some other momentary hero.

At the appointed time, after weeks of preliminary preparations for the great parade, all boats dress ship and mill around at some quiet rendezvous location. Exactly on the scheduled hour (another impossible dream) the designated lead boat, having previously run the course as planned, moves out slowly while the other boats sort themselves out and fall in astern, about three boat-lengths apart. Speed must be well coordinated and distances evenly maintained by a parade marshall buzzing around in a little speedboat. He bird-dogs the fleet with appropriate entreaties to shape up. The VIP who reviews the show will be provided with a craft or shoreside platform large enough for his party of aides and spouses to be reasonably comfortable and near the center of land spectators. A thoughtful touch is to have the parade marshal take up station opposite the reviewing boat and run the parade down between the two, the marshal speaking over a suitable channel to the loudspeaker ashore with a running commentary about each boat as it approaches.

The method of rendering and answering salutes will, of course, depend upon the high or low degree of the whole affair, whether it be a serious and respectful memorial, civic advertising, or just holiday exuberance. In general, as explained in Chapter 3, military formality is seldom suited to modern yacht routine. Ensigns are no longer dippable; bareheaded, albeit earnest, hand salutes would bring out the worst in any self-respecting drill sergeant, and non-reg arm-waving would very likely include raised beer cans as well. Perhaps the rules should settle for a breast salute rendered by all hands except the helmsman from wherever there is room to stand without rocking the boat. The VIPs and Apple Queens can reply according to their mood.

New-Member Recognition

The annual welcoming of new members can be a most effective part of bringing these newcomers into club activities. Some clubs simply give a conducted tour of club facilities and let it go at that; others may put on a banquet where all hands and spouses are briefly introduced, and officers give redundant welcoming speeches. Either of these rather routine gestures misses out on the potential opportunity for the appropriate communication that such an occasion presents. Perhaps less like an ordinary party but undoubtedly more effective in conveying club policies and spirit is a special meeting where not only officers give their welcoming words, but the chairman of each committee gives his story and opens the door to that activity or function.

Certificates of membership are presented at this meeting, together with club books and rosters and such souvenir publications as the size of the initiation fee may warrant. These take-home trophies should be of a quality befitting the club.

Trophies

A goodly measure of the fun that goes with trophies and awards is their presentation. We recall the classic way a jewelry store displays its diamond rings: black velvet and a spotlight. Trophies, silverware, and plaques deserve the full treatment. They look stunning when properly displayed. And, each presentation deserves description and a full recounting of the exploits of the proud award recipient. If the club has established certain customs, they need to be carried along. Even some newly inspired performances can be the making of a tradition. An example is the sudden whimsy of an outgoing commodore of an old New England club, some years ago, who removed his outmoded uniform jacket and handed it to his successor together with appropriate words of praise and good wishes. That same coat is now exhumed from mothballs at every change of watch. The blue serge and the multiple black braid trefoil stripes are always a pleasant glimpse of the old days—a tradition.

Many of the yachting trophies that carry the most prestige follow the tradition of the old "America's Cup," that ornate "ould mug" of Tom Lipton's futile dreams— that is, named for the winning vessel herself. Other worthy trophy names are in the category of memorials to individuals or those bearing the titles of clubs or public officers, and are all in good taste.

Any member who feels that a little more recognition should be made available to that more or less silent majority, the cruising skippers, or even something for the "social" members, is always entitled to think up some pleasant oddity for annual recognition and name the cup for himself. That automatically gets his name headlined, a common and quite acceptable practice. The trick is to think up some achievement not already well provided with suitable recognition.

Posting the Flag

Posting of the flag at meetings can be completely overlooked or it can take on the boring complications of medieval monks at prayer. Display of the flag of the United States at indoor meetings ashore is prescribed by Public Law 928, adopted by Congress in 1944:

> When displayed from a staff on the speaker's platform, the United States flag should occupy the position of honor at the speaker's right as he faces the audience. Any other flag . . . on the platform should be placed at the speaker's left. But when the U. S. flag is displayed on a staff elsewhere than on a platform it shall be placed in the position of honor at the right of the audience as they face the platform.
>
> When displayed flat against a wall, either horizontally or vertically, the union should be to the left as viewed by the audience.

CHAPTER SIX

WHAT'S IN A NAME?

THE fascinating question of "What's in a name?" now
and then occurs in classic philosophy. Usually the
philosopher is speculating about a reputation. But what
we have in mind here is the registered name to be spelled
out in proud gold leaf, or reasonable facsimile thereof, on
the boat's stern; the name which visibly transforms a hulk
from *it* to *she* and gives her personality.

Many, and frequently foolish, are the reasons why a
boat, particularly a pleasure boat, is feminine. Male chau-
vinists seem to think that she needs their strong hand on
the tiller to curb her wayward ways; those of more realistic outlook see the female grace and charm, the true
companion. Each one may have a point. It would seem
that any decent boat of a design not too antagonistic to the
sea is *she* to the honest skipper who has learned, as have I
and many others before me, that, rather like my First
Mate of many years, her strengths sometimes exceed my
understanding; her frailties, more often, reflect my own
mistakes.

The very fact that many boats today are mass-produced, and look as much alike as cars, makes naming—the conferring of a bit of individuality—even more important. The ideal name must (1) please the owner and his family, (2) be generally appropriate to the type of boat, and (3) communicate easily to others. This process of thinking of a just-right name, like any thinking unaided by sudden inspiration, can be a chore, even futile, if one neglects to start with a reasonable set of assumptions. One way to start is to recall those fleeting visions which impelled her purchase in the first place, thoughts that drifted by during private fantasies about the boat. Unlike the naming of a daughter, dreams invoking mood or alluding to natural phenomena are quite acceptable: *Orion, Aeolus, Nocturne, Wanderer, North Star, Buccaneer.* References to one's occupation or hobby may be just the thing: *Saltprint, Blue Chip, Twenty Twenty, Off Call, Gourmet;* or even a play on your name. And of course, the cherished name of wife, daughter, girl friend, or cousin Susie Q. conveys quite well the affection which includes the boat within our family circle.

Lloyd's Register of American Yachts, once the great "peek book" of pleasure boating, listed about ten thousand boats but only two thousand different names, which seems to indicate the popularity of certain favorite dreams such as those beginning with "Sea" or "Lady" and the dozens of *Spindrifts, Quests,* and *Kittiwakes.* Since names are not subject to copyright, we are free to seize whatever one we like and make it ours. However, there has to be a minor satisfaction in some degree of personal

NAUTICAL ETIQUETTE AND CUSTOMS

exclusiveness, when it's not too far out. A most important test for suitability of any name is to speak it on the radio. If it cannot be quickly understood, and understood correctly, forget it. Also, names contrived from anagrams are frequently without much meaning to a stranger. Comic names soon lose their impact and get tiresome. Would the busy watchstander at the Coast Guard Station, listening to several channels all at once, recognize the name? Imagine putting out a Mayday call, shouting: "*Thisisit*, I need assistance." Comes the reply:

> "Vessel calling Coast Guard, what is your name?"
> "*Thisisit*. I'm sinking."
> "I read you, Cap, but what is your name?"

We hope such urgent exchange with the Coast Guard will never occur, but the yacht's name will still go out on the air at the beginning and end of every radio conversation. The FCC makes no bones about it. With required and incessant repetition, wisecracks are no longer wise and oral oddities are forever being twisted by puzzled listeners. *Gaberlunzie* or *Cle-Ill-Ahee* are just big trouble; *Kwalgurle*, *Drambuie*, and *More Bad News* are guaranteed to become embarrassing. Lengthy names are always nuisances, more ridiculed than remembered, to say nothing of the space problems they present. *John Van Oldenbarneveldt* will forever be referred to as "that boat with the Flying Dutchman name," and marine operators, skillful as they are in telephone semantics, will skip the whole historic mouthful and settle for a garbled substitute, probably *John Smith*. The disillusioned owner has two options: he paints out the funny name and signs a lot of forms to change it, or he sells the boat and lets the next man sign the forms.

Lettering

It takes skilled hands to do a proper job of lettering. Most yards have some good professional on call who can also advise on size and type of lettering for good contrast and visibility. For a do-it-yourself job, plastic letters serve fairly well. They are removable when refinishing the hull, also much less expensive than gold leaf—and they look it. Nothing equals professional handlettering unless it be a carved name board. On more expensive craft, especially on nostalgic character boats, a sculptured name board embellished with exotic scrolls carved by an artist speaks clearly of classic elegance.

As stated in the present bylaws of many clubs, "Each enrolled yacht shall have her name legible on the outside of her stern." That requirement is still valid because "stern" rather than "transom" is specified. Many transoms today are cluttered with outboard motors or are blocked from view by ladders or low-slung dinghies. These situations where the transom is not readily visible require that the name be lettered on each quarter, as on double-enders. And legibility also means a type of lettering quickly readable. Also at the stern, below the name but slightly smaller, goes the hailing port; not a postal address, just the port of registry for documented yachts or the home port for numbered boats. This should be checked with the local Coast Guard Auxiliary inspector. It is important to remember that binoculars are frequently being focused on that name and hailing port.

Labeling of Appurtenances

Displaying the yacht's name on sidelight screens, although not required, still remains a proud custom and is well adapted to flying bridge sides. In this location miniatures in color of private signal and club burgee with crossed staffs painted above the name are a quiet touch of quality. At the opposite extreme are advertising trademarks touting Whale Gut Oil or Hell Fire Spark Plugs.

The yacht complete with name now has status as an individual with full rights to property all her own. She can even be sued. Therefore, all of her appurtenances, her life rings, fenders, cradle, mooring buoy, dinghy, and, for cruising boats, even the stationery, are hers and should be lettered with her name. This has always been the classic custom among the cognoscenti and so remains. Good yards see to these details automatically, but some lesser yards catering to novice owners will overlook these marks of personal assurance. They tend to use the owner's name, perhaps to simplify their bookkeeping, slapping his name on cradle, buoy, or slip-space instead of recognizing the true entity, the boat herself. They have to be instructed, even cajoled, to provide this simple touch of elegance. Also in these times of thievery, it makes good sense to mark all items, and it might as well be done in style. To see an owner's name painted on a slip or mooring buoy infers that it is he, not she, who gets tied up there. If this fine old custom has slipped somewhat, it's not for reasons of new technology; it's simply that a hurried world forgets that "club membership" is indicated in many subtle ways. The United States Yacht Racing Union regulations governing the standards for yachts in all sanctioned races (except the afternoon affairs close to shore) require that the vessel's name be legible on all miscellaneous buoyant equipment such as life jackets, oars, cushions, fenders, rafts, etc. And, merely as an afterthought, it might be comforting to know that after shipwreck, some tragic bit of cockpit grating lettered *Chloe* will mutely end the Coast Guard search.

Dinghy Naming

Some owners seem to feel an obligation to contrive a separate dinghy name, a cute diminutive perhaps. Some of these aren't bad at all. For instance, the schooner *Salty Dog* has a dinghy labeled *Hot Dog*. On the other hand, the owner of the cruiser *Sea Dog* named his dinghy *Bitch*. Maybe he was right, but why tell the world? The cruiser *Mistress* has a dinghy labeled *Love Child,* and the lovely cutter *Cadenza* has a tender lettered *Coda.*

But in general, a proper dinghy displays its mother's name for the simple reason that it is one of her appurtenances. It is part of her equipment, covered by the same insurance, included in her inventory, and she therefore states it clearly. However, the name, applied with lettering to suit the size and style of the little craft, is placed inside, usually on the transom's forward face where it is visible when tied up at a float. If there is an outboard motor (some skippers are rediscovering oars), the name is kept clear of motor clamps even if it's necessary to etch it on the after thwart. Oars, so easily borrowed, must have the name carved or burned in near the grips.

The increasing popularity of "inflatables" for dinghy service needs special attention. Quite understandably, in this age of high-production sameness, many of these rubber doughnuts display only the name of some strange ship named *Avon.* Admittedly, the grace and beauty aspects of tradition have little place in utilitarian departures such as this. But the very practical advantages of inflatables in many cases have made them popular and their use as dinghies doubtless will continue to increase. They may not look like boats but they most certainly perform that function, at least when the wind isn't blowing. Therefore, as a tender for its mother ship, it must be labeled accordingly. The name is applied wherever there is solid surface visible from dockside. It is put on with rubber paint or with contrasting rubber letters glued to thwartship tubes. This gives the thing its due identity. After all, it is most assuredly an inventory item of a very special ship.

Many little sailboats, Turnabouts and Lasers, Sunfish, and the like, may be only one of thousands in their class but they may be little gems of naval architecture. The same is true of many little outboards. Skippered by a youngster who is learning what the sport is all about, each deserves a personal identity beyond the class and number

on the sail or the maker's number plate. Let's allow the kids an opportunity to express themselves and watch these younger sailors develop into "members of the club." And let parental guidance be uncompromising, with no exceptions, that the wearing of PFDs (personal flotation devices) while messing about in boats is always good form.

CHAPTER SEVEN

GUESTS AND "MEMBERS OF THE CLUB"

THE larger clubs with extensive shore and waterfront facilities have rules which detail guest privileges and their sponsor's responsibilities. Some clubs split hairs by having one set of rules for "guests" and another for "visitors." Most clubs don't bother with defining the difference unless the frequency of these nonmember privileges gets out of hand. This problem is discussed below under The Skipper's Burdens.

The Guest Book

Any club with a membership larger than that in which all hands have a close acquaintanceship with each other is too large to skip the formalities of a guest book or register. Every member who brings a friend to lunch or a group to any other entertainment or facility; every member who invites a friend or group of friends to come aboard his boat to help him race or enjoy a cruise; every member who for any reason invites a nonmember to the clubhouse, parking area, or waterfront facilities must be requested to have these guests sign and date the guest book. It is most helpful in formulating club policy.

The club must analyze how best to meet its members' needs in providing privileges for guests of members. Dues must always be justified by maintaining a fair degree of exclusivity in the use and benefits of facilities. At the same time, an important benefit of any membership is the use of facilities in connection with the member's private entertaining as an individual host. It is also the whole membership's obligation to assess itself sufficiently to maintain these benefits of membership.

Club bylaws must clearly specify special charges, if any, for the use of certain named facilities. Other, more general and indefinite, privileges must be controlled by specific bylaws regulating type of use and the frequency with which members may share club privileges with nonmembers. A guest book thus not only helps in formulating club policy but is also essential as an unobtrusive reminder of the existence of the rules.

The Skipper's Burdens

Marrying romantic couples was once considered by the landbound laity as a captain's most exalted function. Today's somewhat more sophisticated boating dilettante adds three more chores: (1) cleaning out the head, (2) providing plenty of ice, and (3) going down with the ship.

But even this realistic job description somehow falls short of including the large cloak of responsibility worn, sometimes unwittingly, by every skipper in either of the two broad categories of pleasure boating: racing and cruising. Each type both burdens and rewards the skipper in ways exclusive to itself. House and racing rules are simply codes of conduct for gentlemanly behavior as accepted in the present day and need no general overhauling from that standpoint provided they are understood and followed by the general membership.

A good racing skipper is the leader of a team. His luck in holding good crewmates depends upon his skill in their training, in providing good equipment, and in his sharing of the glory, if any. His reputation and responsibilities also include the shoreside behavior of his crew, especially around the clubhouse. A common burden is the not uncommon intrusion of the deck-ape types who gravitate to the winning boats and owners with their generous perquisites. They can trim sails and handle coffee grinders to perfection, but around the club they may be prone to assuming guest status and then flouting its code. Naturally, feathers get ruffled. The unpleasantness might well be avoided were the club guest book always signed and understood by every visitor. Such visitors are not exclusively the members of another club which is granted reciprocity, or personal friends invited to lunch by a member; they may just be present with automatic-guest status by virtue of their role in any function in which the host club is participating. This would include the skipper-owner of any boat entered in a club event, regardless of any other club affiliation. His signature tacitly implies guest-of-the-club status.

103

The owner-skipper's amateur crew, however, should sign the book as crew and guests of the owner and be so regarded for the duration of the event only. Responsibility is thus designated and this guest skipper assumes full responsibility for his crew while around the club.

Sir Edward Heath of Her Majesty's Privy Council, longtime prime minister and, most important to yachtsmen, a world class racing skipper, was noted not only for the talent and teamwork of his crew afloat but especially for their loyalty in reflecting his image ashore. His crew had absorbed by training and example a pride in themselves, a self-esteem both unobtrusive and verbally restrained, and, as Gilbert and Sullivan put it, would "never never use a big, big D." Well hardly ever!

Frequent or continuing events such as local weekly races which involve the presence of local but nonclub members as crew can quite easily put a strain on guest rules and definitions. Many a weekly afternoon race is sailed with a single club member skipper and a crew of freeloaders, all of whom continue to enjoy club privileges and facilities before, during, and after their racing recreation. The problem is a real one. The owner-member's boat can't be raced without his well-trained crew. His membership undoubtedly includes a spouse, but not his pals who make his racing possible.

The club bylaws must state something to the effect that guest privileges are specifically limited as to extent and frequency, a necessary convention toward making membership worthwhile. Poorly managed clubs may have no such bylaw at all or, if they do, it may simply be ignored. Whatever the local situation, the problem must be faced and answered fairly lest the club find itself swamped with a horde of nonpaying "members."

Tipping

While officially forbidden in any respectable club, tipping is impossible to eliminate entirely. Nevertheless, it can and should be controlled and administered fairly to provide the same incentive that tipping is supposed to foster. A policy of adding a standard gratuity, say fifteen percent, to dining room and bar checks works very well. Outside and waterfront help may receive a year-end bonus from a fund of voluntary contributions. All these funds may be administered and apportioned by the manager most directly concerned.

Fortunately, the old requirement of tipping messboys and stewards will seldom arise. These worthies have become an endangered species, along with sideboys in whites. The professional captain is still around but we do not tip yacht captains; they get their gratuities from chandleries or maintenance firms—a hallowed custom.

Dress Codes

Time was, not too long ago, when yachts carried uniformed crews who did all the actual sailing while their splendidly attired owners and guests viewed with their binoculars the distant race and its maneuvers from the armchairs of the clubhouse. The garb of all hands was

specified according to the day and function, just as were the hours and places where women might set foot if properly escorted by a male attired in the regulation mess jacket.

Prior to World War II, yachting still retained its royal heritage. Yachtsmen played the game with uniforms prescribed for every rank and situation. Uniforms "A," "B," "C," or "D" were required for admission to clubrooms and functions, for day or evening, ashore or afloat. Of course, it was a gorgeous scene. But it was playacting even then, and the script, word-for-word, is still printed in the lengthy bylaws of some "play navy" clubs—largely ignored, to be sure, but still there for those who crave to be correct. A standard wording still in print reads: "The club shall prescribe uniforms to be worn by members and the crews of members' yachts." The club specifies the service dress of double-breasted sack coat, waistcoat, trousers, necktie, club buttons, and type and color of the cloth. The same but even more detailed for those now-historic mess jackets, cloaks, caps, and shoes, plus special uniforms and rating marks for the professionals of deck, engineer, and steward departments. For club officers and members too, the trefoil sleeve braid, black on blues, white on whites, the cap device, and every grade of foul anchor ornament is seriously spelled out. Gilbert and Sullivan set it all to music in *H. M. S. Pinafore*. These club bylaws without the music leave something to be desired.

Here and there a self-respecting club dining room insists that shoes and some sort of jacket shall be worn, at least at evening meals. But at other times the scene is all too often every man (and woman) for himself (or herself), according to his own degree of personal rebellion. There seems to be no single trend. Some like red pants, some have adopted the compact Thomas Lipton cap, a minor go-to-hell gesture. Dock boys at marinas favor regulation white-top navy caps. All of this is added proof that people don't go "yachting" any more; they go cruising, or they just go out for a sail or to putter in the greatest comfort possible. The neatness of khaki pants and shirt complete with black necktie frequently distinguishes the professional captain on larger craft from the shorts-clad, hairy-chested owner.

If the board of governors feels the need of regulations for members' clothing, let it be guided by the possible and practical lest its wishful taste for uniforms and stripes be observed only by the graying, armchair types. As for the rules for clothing when afloat, the days of regulation and formality have vanished with the comedy of overstuffed importance.

Some clubs still slumber in an unreal world of the past. In the yearbook of the good old Boston Yacht Club it states flatly: "Ladies are not allowed in the Taproom at any time." But yearbooks still are printed to be exchanged with other clubs, not really for compliance by the membership.

The only areas where uniforms are required in the better clubs today are for employees in the dining room and for those providing outside and waterfront services. The word "uniform" in this case does not mean elaborate or showy dress. It very definitely does mean, however, a similarity for purposes of recognition and a type and style suited to performing the intended job with neat and clean appearance.

Standard shirts and pants of one specified color, commonly sold as work clothing, is ideal for dock attendants, launch captains, grounds keepers, and other outside help. Dining room waiters and waitresses can be clothed in matching outfits, usually from off-the-shelf items. Such outfits, although ready-made and of low cost, can easily be personalized with an appliqued miniature of the club burgee and possibly a name. Simple and appropriate as are uniforms of this practical sort, they do improve morale among the hands and convey a pride of membership among the afterguard.

Beyond the Clubhouse

Afloat, the cruising couple has no written rules of etiquette other than the good manners implied in boiling down such regulations as those of the Rules of the Nautical Road. But, perhaps all safety regulations contain a large measure of required politeness. Special safety regulations, as propounded by the Cruising Club of America for its members, as well as those basics required by the U. S. Coast Guard, such as fire extinguishers, life jackets, flares, engine ventilation, etc., are a bare minimum. Many yacht clubs add their own particular requirements for safe operation by any boat entitled to fly the club burgee. For example, the New York Yacht Club requires that any boat enrolled in that club's fleet shall, among other things, "be fully capable of accompanying the fleet on a cruise along the Atlantic seaboard."

Strangely, the U. S. Power Squadrons, dedicated to nautical education, have no safety standards of their own, and their ensign flies from whatever craft a member can contrive to keep afloat.

Providing safety on commercial craft is mandatory, but on private boats (those not for hire) safety is largely in the thoughtfulness-and-good-manners category. Guests are left to make some large assumptions, but they are certainly entitled to a thorough introduction to the boat's facilities and the philosophy behind its operation. Guests should know the where and how of PFDs (personal flotation devices) and fire-fighting apparatus, the rules for fuel stops, and what, if any, deck locations are off-limits while under way.

Many operators of small boats, outboards especially, not only show some disregard for man-made laws regarding speed and wake and right of way, but they also tend quite frequently to challenge nature's laws of boat stability. In small boats lacking forward cockpits, guests and children should be forbidden to ride the bow while under way. The immediate danger is quite apparent, but the hidden danger lies in the effect of added bow weight on the hull's ability to rise to waves. Even with a deep and well-guarded forward cockpit the skipper must know enough to balance off his speed against his forward load. Before the skipper can explain these properties of natural law to his guests, he must have given them some thought himself. Allowing a guest to be in real jeopardy of falling overboard or allowing poor weight distribution aboard can hardly be considered as being a proper host. By the same token, it might be wise to explain that small boats are very responsive to shifts of weight, and a person's sudden movement could have an equally sudden effect on the boat's stability.

The racing skipper's more or less silent counterpart in the larger and more varied field, lumped as "cruising," may wear any of half a dozen different hats. The term encompasses both sail and power, afternoon or offshore passages, fishing trips or family outings, or simply having friends aboard while anchored. In general, he is more relaxed, without the urgency and tension of racing, but frequently with even more responsibility. For not only must the boat and all equipment be in shipshape order but the guests, while doubtless good company, may very likely not be overly familiar with the customs of the boating scene nor with the boat itself, its facilities, and its mysterious navigation.

Still another responsibility of the cruising skipper which, alas, is all too often overlooked, is the behavior of his vessel and crew when at anchor. Today's harbors are horrendously overcrowded, sometimes wall-to-wall boats, as people try to escape to a quiet refuge from the noise and confusion ashore. It takes skill and experience to anchor so as not to foul your neighbor's rode—or shower him with sparks from your charcoal grill—or bruise his topsides in the midnight shift of wind or tide. All too often the beauty of a lovely harbor is shattered by the interminable thumping of a powerboat's generator as its

111

crew watches TV into the wee small hours, or blasts the welkin with its 300-watt stereo system. Just as frustrating is the crew that has become addled on Mount Gay rum and bombards the harbor with ear-splitting guffaws, risque jokes, and off-key singing. The behavior of such boats and crews is a direct reflection on the poor seamanship of their skippers and their selfish disregard for those who have vainly sought the peace and sanctuary of a quiet harbor.

Guests Afloat

Overnight guests involve additional bits of thoughtfulness, coping with the head, stowing gear, and assigning duties and suggestions as to the ship's routine.

In addition to providing themselves with their boating clothes and foul weather gear, male guests should be prepared for the possibility of going ashore to dine at a jacket-and-necktie type of club. This eventuality could also be an opportunity for the guest to pay the check. For women clothing is casual and there is rarely an occasion for heels. But it is wise for guests and skipper and mate to talk it over and keep dress simple. Then everything should be taken aboard in a soft carrier with the fragile gifts for bar or galley rolled up in the soft clothing. It is important to keep in mind that what builders blithely advertise as "wardrobes" in their boats are usually no more than crevices with doors—hence the nautical term "locker."

Relationships between hosts and guests are best when all hands speak a common language—words and terms that indicate an understanding of the subject. Every sport has its own vocabulary, and boating is no exception. Indeed, more words have been outmoded and dropped from the nautical vocabulary than still exist in the jargon of all other sports combined, but certain words still in current usage mark the speech of "members of the club." It is written that in 1698 Peter the Great paid a visit to England and soon demonstrated that no true yachtsman can be all bad. Macaulay records that:

> Peter the Great found the only Englishman in whose society he seemed to take much pleasure was the commoner, Caemarthan, whose passion for the sea bore some resemblance to his own, and who was very competent to give an opinion about every part of a ship from stem to stern, in terms familiar to the brotherhood.

If we are guests, our ears need to be attuned to these keys to the brotherhood. We should notice, for example, that the host does not show the guest a "bathroom" but rather the nautical "head" and its special features.

Ability to recognize some common types of boats is a phase of etiquette somewhat more advanced perhaps than knowing when the sun has reached yardarm level, but it adds a lot to our enjoyment. The owner of a Huckins cruiser may become morose if his guest compliments him on his Chris-Craft, and vice versa. It is a good idea to know the difference between yawl and ketch, sloop and cutter, knots and miles per hour, and to know what is meant by rope, line, anchor rode, and painter.

The skipper will, of course, have provided all the legal and advisable equipment but in addition will explain and demonstrate them all including the boat's conveniences and the little pet devices that every well-cared-for boat acquires.

In general, the skipper and his first mate run the whole show in cruising craft. They do the chores, get the meals, and clean things up. There's enough variety to intrigue and offer opportunity for any guests to be helpful. But what is helpful may appear quite differently to owners than to guests. The owner-skipper, as a host, by his own example allows the guest to savor the enjoyment of proper handling of the boat and all her gadgets. The guest, of course, is duty bound to learn these rites and also to keep smiling about the lousy bunks and lack of privacy, to keep his gear well stowed and out of the way, and never be seasick to windward.

The skipper should provide the opportunity to give the guest the exquisite pleasure of handling the helm while the skipper conns. Few people seem to realize that even the greatest and most powerful ships, Navy, Coast Guard, or merchant, are steered by an enlisted helmsman while an officer always conns the ship. Sam Cunard demanded that his captains be good hosts but reminded them that "passengers would be well aware of when his presence on the bridge would be preferable to his socializing in the grand saloon."

Sometimes it's quite surprising to discover the innocence of things nautical among our occasional guests (even among some boat owners whose interest is not so much in boats as such as in the fishing). They may be happily unaware of Rules of the Nautical Road or unfamiliar with the use of nautical charts and compass. It is a pity. They know not what they're missing. Therefore we need not only to be tolerant but also rather careful to provide a conning officer when giving these amateurs the pleasure of the helm.

Of endless fascination to the novice guest is that marvelous device, the compass. Had this simple instrument been recently developed it would have been hailed as space-age technology. But since its origin is shrouded in the mists of early witchcraft and anticlerical black arts, all we need to know today is that it works beautifully for those who speak its language. Unencumbered by the needless mystery fostered by bemused instructors, the guest can be a compass-using expert in less than fifteen minutes. When the skipper asks his guest to take the helm and hold a compass course, he can use his judgment as to whether it is an appropriate time to give some instruction. If simply holding a course is quite enough of a challenge, so be it; let the instruction await another time. But if the novice helmsman is up to it, the skipper can explain the difference between the true course and the compass course. Let's say, for example, that the true or geographic course is Zero Nine Zero degrees in an area that has a five degree variation east. The effect of this, of course, is that to hold a true course, the helmsman must hold a compass course that is five degrees less—in this case, Zero Eight Five.

As you might expect, mariners have a little rhyme for this, a memory aid, that says if the variation, or error, is east, the compass is always, "least," or less; and any error west means compass "best," or greater than the true course.

The novice is now privy to a mystery of the ages!

Since piloting is best performed in a tranquil atmosphere, guests must let the helmsman concentrate. Long-winded stories should be saved for the anchorage because two pairs of eyes are needed to focus on the business of the moment. Sam Cunard's directive: "There shall always be two officers on watch" is a fundamental that doubles the enjoyment of cruising yachtsmen of today. It is no ancient whimsy that navy custom also calls for repetition by the helmsman of every steering order. Not to be confused with "backseat driving," this double watch is obligatory in any well-run and happy ship. A guest will welcome the feeling of responsibility. The helmsman of the moment, even though he may anticipate it, should quietly repeat the command. It is professional.

Keep in Touch

A courtesy too often overlooked is the maintenance of regular contact with home or club, especially to avoid alarm or being posted overdue. When a schedule has been planned, even tentatively, a failure to arrive as planned can be very worrisome to family and friends and may set off an expensive Coast Guard search, even though we may not be worth all that trouble. Frequently a cruising boat may choose to sit out a time of foul weather in some unscheduled cove rather than attempt the discomfort of making the scheduled port. Such common-sense good judgment is indeed commendable, but the failure to inform those who might be worried is difficult to excuse.

Again Sam Cunard: "When overtaken by foul weather, under no circumstances are you to move your vessel from where she may be lying safely." But he didn't say that you shouldn't tell somebody where you are.

* * *

Boating spreads its own rewards among all types and temperaments, from competitors who thrive on tension to those who seek relief from daily pressures; from kids who get afloat in little cat boats to graying circumnavigators; from speed enthusiasts to those who revel in their comforts, "the way of a ship" has it all.

APPENDICES

A Suggested Yacht Routine for Clubs

U. S. Power Squadron Flag Code

*U. S. Coast Guard Auxiliary
Flag Code for Power Vessels*

A SUGGESTED YACHT ROUTINE
FOR CLUBS

Section I: Flags and Signals

All yachts qualified for enrollment in the XYC Squadron according to the type, size, and safety standards set forth in Chapter — of the bylaws, when in commission, shall observe the following flag routine at such times between 0800 and sunset as the yacht is manned and weather permitting:

(1) Ensign

When moored or at anchor the American Yacht Ensign shall be displayed from either the stern staff or from the afterpeak as convenient to the type of rig, except when racing. Outboard launches and sail craft with overhanging booms may locate the stern staff off center on the starboard side.

(2) Burgee

(a) Mastless and single-masted craft with a bow staff, at the bow staff. If no bow staff, at the truck.

(b) Yachts with two or more masts, at the foremost truck.

(3) Private Signal

(a) Single-masted yachts with bow and stern staffs, at the truck.

(b) Yachts with two or more masts, at the mast next aft of the foremost mast.

(c) Mastless craft may fly the Private Signal from a vertical radio antenna when the Yacht Ensign and Club Burgee are being flown from stern and bow staffs respectively.

120

(4) Officers' Flags

A Flag Officer shall display his flag when on board in the place and instead of his private signal or, in the case of a single-masted sailing yacht, instead of the burgee, 0800 to sunset, except when racing or when displaying the burgee of another club or the race committee's flag.

(5) Fleet Captain's Flag

The Fleet Captain may display his flag when on board in the place and instead of his private signal, or at the port spreader, except when racing or when displaying the burgee of another club or the race committee's flag.

(6) Race Committee Flag

On a yacht acting as race committee boat, the committee's flag shall be displayed at the main truck in place of any other flag. Launches acting as committee boats shall erect a jury-rigged mainmast.

(7) Union Jack

The Union Jack may be used in a dress ship hoist or flown from a port spreader, afloat or at the shore station mast.

(8) Night or Wind Pennant

A blue pennant may be displayed at the main truck when no other flags are flown.

(9) Other Flags

Flags authorized by recognized yachting organizations may be displayed at option in accordance with their respective regulations provided that the Club Burgee shall be flown as directed in Section I (2) when in the Club anchorage or float area. The display of Owner Absent and Owner's Meal Flag or Crew's Meal Pennant is discouraged. The Guest Flag may be flown from the starboard main spreader when the yacht is under charter. The port spreader may be used as the place for any flags not specifically designated herein.

(10) Racing

While racing, yachts shall comply with the Racing Rules and any specific instructions of the race committee.

(11) Size of Flags

(a) The Yacht Ensign should be between three-quarters of an inch and one inch on the fly for each foot of overall length of the yacht.

(b) The Burgee, Private Signal, and Officer's Flag should be at least three-eighths of an inch on the fly for each foot of overall length or mast height. Hoist shall be two-thirds the fly.

(12) Order of Colors

When making colors shorthanded, the Ensign shall be hoisted first, followed by the Club Burgee and the Private Signal. Flags are lowered in reverse order.

Section II: Lights

Searchlights shall be handled carefully and in such a way as not to be objectionable to others. Anchor and running lights shall be displayed in compliance with legal regulations. The display of Owner Absent and Meal lights is discouraged as are also lights designating rank.

Section III: Salutes and Ceremonies

(a) On ceremonial occasions the breast salute is authorized. Yachts in passing shall not salute other than the arm-wave greeting.

(b) The shore station shall mark the time of colors with one gun.

(c) On the Fourth of July and when ordered for other occasions, a yacht, when manned and weather permitting, shall dress ship during the hours designated.

(d) On the death of a yacht owner, his Private Signal shall be half-masted from the port yardarm of the shore station mast from 0800 to sunset on the day of death announcement when the Club is in commission. The Club Burgee may also be half-masted.

(e) On days of national mourning, the Yacht Ensign at the shore station shall be half-masted from 0800 to 1200.

Section IV: Shore Stations

The mast is considered as the aftermast of a vessel standing out to sea. Colors shall be made in all weather while the Club is in commission.

(a) The American Yacht Ensign is displayed at the peak if there is a gaff, otherwise at the masthead.

(b) The Burgee, on masts with a gaff, at the masthead. On masts without a gaff, at the starboard yardarm. On bare masts, on the same hoist and below the Yacht Ensign at the masthead.

(c) The flag of the senior officer present is displayed from the starboard yardarm. The flag of a visiting officer, the Union Jack, or an informative flag may be flown from the port yardarm.

UNITED STATES POWER SQUADRON FLAG CODE

Flag	When flown	Powerboat with bow and stern staffs only	Powerboat with bow and stern staffs and single mast	Single-masted sailing yacht	Powerboat or sailing yacht with two masts
U.S. ensign or U.S. yacht ensign[1]	0800 to sundown[5]	Stern staff[3]	Stern staff[3]	At anchor or under way: from stern staff (except when racing). Optional: from peak if gaff-rigged, or from leech of mainsail if Marconi-rigged[4].	At anchor or under way: from stern staff (except when racing). Optional: from afterpeak if gaff-rigged, or from leech of aftermost sail if Marconi-rigged[4].
USPS ensign[1]	0800 to sundown[5]	Stern staff[3]	Stern staff or starboard yardarm[2 & 3]	As above	As above
Squadron pennant or yacht club burgee	0800 to sundown[5]	Bow staff	Bow staff	At bow staff if yacht so equipped, otherwise at the truck	Foremost truck
Flag officer's (rectangular)	Day and night while boat is in commission	Not flown	At the truck instead of private signal	At the truck instead of squadron pennant or yacht club burgee	Aftermost truck instead of private signal
Appointed officer's (swallowtail)	0800 to sundown[5]	Not flown	At the truck instead of private signal	At the truck instead of squadron pennant or yacht club burgee	Aftermost truck instead of private signal
USPS past officer's signal	0600 to sundown[5]	Not flown	At the truck	At the truck	Aftermost truck
Private signal	0800 to sundown[5]	Not flown	At the truck	At the truck	Aftermost truck
Union Jack	0800 to sundown. At anchor only, on Sundays and holidays or when dressing ship[5]	Not flown	Not flown	Not flown	Jack staff
Guest flag	0800 to sundown when owner is absent, but guests are on board[5]	Not flown	Starboard yardarm	Starboard spreader spreader	Starboard main
Officer-in-Charge (OIC) pennant	Day and night during activity for which authorized	Not flown	At the truck, above officer's flag	At the truck, above officer's flag	Aftermost truck, above officer's flag

1   A USPS member has the option of flying the U. S. ensign, the U. S. yacht ensign, or the USPS ensign.

2   If the USPS ensign is flown from the yardarm, the U. S. ensign or the U. S. yacht ensign should be flown from the stern staff.

3   On boats with outboard motors and on sailing yachts with overhanging booms, the stern staff to be located to starboard of motor or boom.

4   Approximately two-thirds of the length of the leech above the clew.

5   Yachts that will be unmanned at color time shall make evening colors beforehand.

Note that where the same hoist is indicated for more than one flag or signal, the choice is optional. The flying of two flags or signals from the same hoist is not authorized, except in the case of the OIC pennant or International Code flags.

U. S. C. G. AUXILIARY FLAG CODE FOR POWER VESSELS

Flag	National ensign	Coast Guard ensign	Auxiliary ensign	Auxiliary officer pennant or burgee	Yacht ensign	USPS ensign	USPS officer flag	Yacht club pennant or unit	Yacht club officer flag	House flag	Gag flags — Meal, etc.
Facility Normal Condition (Status 1)	Stern staff or gaff (Note 1)	No	Truck—bow staff (Note 2) (Note 14)	Stbd. yard—bow staff (Note 3) (Note 6)	No (Note 4)	Stbd. yard only (Note 5)	(Note 6)	Bow staff (Note 10)	Stbd. yard. (Note 6)	No (Note 7)	No (Note 8)
Under Orders (Status 2)	Stern staff or gaff (Note 1)	No	Truck—bow staff (Note 2) (Note 14)	(Note 3) (Note 15)	No (Note 15)	No (Note 15)	No (Note 15)	No (Note 15)	No (Note 15)	No (Note 7)	No (Note 8)
Under Orders USCG Officer Aboard (Status 3)	Stern staff or gaff (Note 1)	Truck (Note 16)	No (Note 16)	No (Note 16)	No (Note 16)	No (Note 16)	No (Note 16)	No (Note 16)	No (Note 16)	No (Note 7)	No (Note 8)
Hours Flown	0800 to sunset	Day and night under orders (Note 13)	Day and night (Note 9)	Officer aboard day and night	0800 to sunset (Note 4)	0800 to sunset (Note 5)	Day and night (Note 6)	0800 to sunset (Note 11)	Day and night (Note 12)	(Note 7)	No

1 **The National Ensign** shall be flown from the stern staff on a power boat except when the vessel is equipped with a gaff, in which case the ensign is flown from the stern staff at anchor, and the gaff when underway.

2 **Auxiliary Ensign**
(a) Shall be flown from the main truck when the vessel is equipped with a mast(s).
(b) Without a mast, from the bow staff.

3 **Auxiliary Officer**—Pennant or burgee shall be flown from the starboard yardarm when the vessel is equipped with a signal mast. If the vessel has no mast, it may be flown in lieu of the Auxiliary ensign from the bow staff. The pennant of a current officer shall take precedence over his own higher ranking past officer's burgee. However, as a matter of courtesy to a visiting officer, display the highest ranking officer flag (pennant or burgee).

4 **The Yacht Ensign**
(a) The flying of the yacht ensign on any yacht, numbered or documented, is neither mandatory nor forbidden.
(b) A documented yacht operating under official orders, becomes a Government vessel, and Government vessels *may not* fly the "Yacht ensign."
(c) All facilities *not documented* shall fly the U.S. ensign, whenever the Auxiliary ensign is flown.

5 **USPS Ensign**—This is the only "service" organization recognized by this code. The USPS ensign may be flown only from the starboard yardarm of a signal mast, *never* from the stern staff or gaff. On facilities flying the Auxiliary ensign, this position of honor is *reserved* for the national ensign.

6 **Officer Flags**—Auxiliary, USPS, yacht or boat club, either pennants or burgees, are flown from the starboard yardarm, except as noted in #3. Only *one* of these flags may be flown at a time.

7 **House Flag**—The owner's private signal known as a house flag is correctly flown at the truck between morning and evening colors; therefore, it *cannot* be flown at the same time as the Auxiliary ensign.

8 **Gag Flags**—Because of the quasi-official status of an Auxiliary facility, cocktail flags, ball-and-chain, or other humorous flags *shall not* be flown when the Auxiliary ensign is flown. Other flags, such as crew's pennant, owner's meal flag, guest flag, absent flag, also shall not be flown with the Auxiliary ensign.

9 **The Auxiliary Ensign**—may be flown *day* and *night* on currently inspected facilities displaying decal, while in commission.

10 **The Yacht Club Pennant**—can be flown from the bow staff.

11 **The Yacht Club Pennant, Flotilla, or Division, Unit Flags**—shall be flown from 0800 to sunset.

12 **Yacht Club Officer Flags**—shall be displayed day and night.

13 **The Coast Guard Ensign**—shall be flown day and night while the facility is under orders with a Coast Guard officer aboard.

14 **No Signal Mast**—When a boat is equipped with a bow and stern staff, and does not have a signal mast, but has a radio antenna, the Auxiliary ensign may be properly displayed by substituting the antenna for a signal mast. The height of the uppermost portion of the Auxiliary ensign should be affixed at a point approximately ⅔ the height of the antenna. *No additional* antennas or outriggers may be utilized.

15 **A Facility Under Official Orders** (Status 2) shall be permitted to fly the Auxiliary officer's pennant or burgee, in addition to the U.S. and Auxiliary ensigns. All other flags—yacht ensign, USPS ensign, yacht club pennants, officer flags, flotilla, division, etc. *shall not* be flown.

16 **Coast Guard Officer Aboard Facilities Under Order** (Status 3) the Coast Guard Ensign substitutes for the Auxiliary ensign; *all* other flags except the national ensign shall be taken down. This includes Auxiliary officer pennants or burgees, yacht ensign, unit flags, USPS ensign, yacht or boat club flags, etc.—only two flags shall be permitted—the national ensign and the Coast Guard ensign.

LINDSAY'S LAW

When your draft exceeds the water's depth,
You are most assuredly aground.